The Age
of Steam

The Age of Steam

The Locomotives, the Railroads, and Their Legacy

John Westwood

THUNDER BAY
P·R·E·S·S

Published in the United States by
Thunder Bay Press
An imprint of the Advantage Publishers Group
5880 Oberlin Drive, Suite 400
San Diego, CA 92121-4794
http://www.advantagebooksonline.com

Produced by
Saraband Inc., PO Box 0032, Rowayton,
CT 06853-0032

ISBN 1-57145-284-2

1 2 3 4 5 6 7 8 9 10

Library of Congress Catolging-in-Publication Data

Westwood, J. N.
    The age of steam / John Westwood.
        p. cm.
    ISBN 1-57145-284-2
    1. Steam locomotives — History. I. Title.

TJ603 .W429 2000
385'.361 — dc21

                                        00-044716

Page 1: *"John Bull," built in England in 1831 for the Camden
& Amboy Railroad. Originally a four-wheeler, it soon received a
leading truck to ease passage over curves. The picture shows it in
later years, after the addition of a glassed-in cab.*

Page 2: *One of the hundreds of American steam locomotives that
have survived into the diesel age. This former freight locomotive
now hauls passenger trains on the Grand Canyon Railroad.*

Below: *Mainline steam traction is still used in China. Here a
passenger and a freight locomotive are serviced at Changchun
locomotive depot.*

FOR GEORGE HALLETT

Contents

Introduction

The steam railroad just managed to touch three centuries. Born when Napoleon Bonaparte was still at large, it remained a significant form of transportation in China at the beginning of the twenty-first century. Elsewhere, the steam locomotive had more or less disappeared during the last half of the twentieth century, as the more economic electric and diesel locomotives replaced it. By the end of that century, with the partial exception of China and a few small pockets of old technology, it was to be seen at work only as part of the tourist and heritage business.

Steam tourist railways attract visitors not only because the sight, sound, and smell of a steam locomotive at work is a lure for the emotions, but because its historic role has long been part of conventional wisdom. Once upon a time, this wisdom says, there was a pre-Railway Age, and then there came the Railway Age, when the power of steam traction transformed society and led directly to the kind of world we live in now: the world of mass production, of going away on vacation, of living in one town and working in another, of making or losing a fortune on the stock exchange, and of big organizations. Above all, a world in which it is seen as quite natural that new technologies should arrive, one after the other, each with the power of enhancing life for some and perhaps ruining it for others.

Just when railroads in the Western world were running their last steam trains, this conventional wisdom came to be challenged. For decades, economic historians had been debating whether the Industrial Revolution was good or bad for the workers, but, having at last squeezed this topic dry, they needed a new controversy and duly found it. University students, having been taught at school the concept that the steam locomotive created modern industrial society, suddenly heard from their instructors that the railroads were not so crucial after all. If actual transportation costs of the Railway Age were compared with what transportation would have cost had there been no railroads, there would not have been a great difference. Therefore, the railroads had not really transformed the economy.

This claim was not so much an attack on conventional wisdom as a challenge to the obvious and, having usefully stimulated discussion and boosted a few academic careers, it soon disappeared from view. It had at least drawn attention to those results of the Railway Age that could not be expressed in figures (and which, therefore, most economists tend

Opposite: The steam locomotive was hard-wearing, but needed constant attention by experienced staff. This remains true on the preserved railroads; here an early twentieth-century locomotive receives attention on the present-day Strasburg Railroad.

Above: "John Stevens," one of six "Crampton Patent" locomotives built in 1849 for the Camden & Amboy Railroad. Their 96-inch driving wheels were located behind the firebox.

to ignore). It was quite easy to show that the steam railroad had not created the Industrial Revolution—factory-made textiles would have come anyway—and that the railroad was not the origin but a feature of that Industrial Revolution, but that was not the main point.

The main point, surely, was that the railroad transformed the way people thought. For better or for worse, the Railway Age was telling them, tomorrow is not going to be like today. The concept of Progress took hold—a concept that the steam locomotive both created and came to symbolize. "Well done steam! Smoke, thou art wonderful, and a reformer!" was how one famous British general expressed it, as early as 1839, after he had been whisked by the London & Birmingham Railway to an urgent interview with the prime minister.

When all is said and done, the main business of the railroads in their first century was the Industrial Revolution. Yet economic historians had a point when they observed that the heavy trains of ore and

coal that were so typical of that time might have been proof of breakneck industrial development, but they were destined for the most part to supply the needs of the railway itself. Like a dog chasing its own tail, the railways were carrying enormous tonnages of fuel and materials that they themselves needed to exist and prosper. This indeed was true at many times and places, but eventually the production capacities built upon the strength of the railroads' demands were deployed elsewhere and were both part and parcel of an expanding economy. Krupp and Vickers, among others, developed their heavy engineering capacities by supplying the railroad industry, and then turned to armaments manufacture.

Essentially, what the steam locomotive did was expand the space in which an individual or a productive enterprise could be active. In pre-railroad societies, a farmer knew that corn could be sent only a certain distance by horse transportation; at some distance, the amount of feed consumed by the horse would equal the load of corn he was pulling. In a horse-driven economy, the only things that could travel long distances were high-value items like prosperous passengers or expensive silks, where transportation costs were a small proportion of the item's value. When the railway came, transportation costs fell enormously, and in economic terms distances shrank. This was not good for everybody; the local shoemaker, for example, no longer enjoyed a monopoly. He lost the stored-up value of his long apprenticeship, as his former clients purchased factory-made shoes carried in by train. They were cheaper, so the customers had money left over to spend on something else, and thus the market grew.

That dispossessed shoemaker had several options. He could go to the workhouse, taking his family with him. He could smarten up his act, so people would still prefer his shoes; he could search for another job, maybe in the expanding railroad business; he might even borrow some money from his friends and start a shoe factory or buy some railway shares. The point was that the world he had known, the secure job for life with its modest income, had been shattered by the steam locomotive, but the new world with all its uncertainties offered great chances for those who could see opportunities and had the will to seize them.

So the age of steam, in its expansive years, was the age of destruction and opportunity. The destruction might fall on small local craftsmen, or on the scores of thousands of tenants expelled onto the streets when railways entered cities, destroying the teeming tenements that stood in their way. It might fall on the peoples of the Plains, like the Native Americans for whom the railroad meant enclosure of land and eventual loss of the previously abundant buffalo herds on which their lifeways depended. It could be the destruction of a prized view, as a huge stone viaduct was thrown across a valley (a century later, descendants of those who clamored against the viaduct would be pleading for its preservation as a heritage monument). Or it could be the destruction of war, because total war, as practiced in the first half of the twentieth century, would have been impossible without the steam railway. Some argued that steam locomotion threatened the destruction of the family, as young ambitious folk left their birthplaces to seek the improved opportunities that mobility gave them. And, of course, there were those who blamed the railways for the destruction of godliness; running trains on Sundays, they said, was a sure call for divine retribution. Since railroad accidents did occur on Sundays, they did not lack ammunition.

Below: A head-on collision suffered by the Maine Central Railroad in 1883. Many such collisions resulted from the misreading of train orders.

Above: A British holiday train, taking passengers from the industrial West Midlands to Devonshire resorts. The locomotive is one of the Great Western Railway's "Castle" class.

while the possibility of train accidents frightened passengers excessively, the high casualty rate of railroad workers did not raise many eyebrows.

The general conclusion was, and remains, that whatever destruction the steam locomotive may have brought was far outweighed by its benefits—the possibilities of experiencing things that were previously undreamed of. Everybody, each in his or her own way, could find new opportunity. For many, the railway provided a well-paid job which, as each recruit acquired new skills, became very secure, because in bad times railways were reluctant to dismiss experienced workers whom they might need again in good times. There was also a section of the workforce that was not employed by the railway but who nevertheless found employment on it—newsboys who roamed the trains selling newspapers and magazines, workers in station restaurants whose all-time elite were the "Harvey Girls" of the American West. In India a sector of the black market was occupied by gleaners of unburned coal, hand-sifted from hot locomotive ash. For these gleaners, who were mainly women, the coming of the diesel locomotive meant a sudden loss of livelihood.

One such Sunday accident occurred near Versailles, France, when a collision, the resulting fire, and the practice of locking passengers into their compartments combined to produce a charred nightmare. Fire, and trapped passengers, would result in Britain's most lethal rail accident during World War I, when two troop trains collided in Scotland near Gretna Green and caught fire, killing more than 200 soldiers. The most lethal American accident for many years occurred in 1887 at Chatsworth, Illinois, when an excursion train ran onto a blazing wooden trestle bridge, collapsing with it. In reality, even in the 1840s, when the Versailles accident occurred, railways were safer than road vehicles in terms of injuries per passenger-mile, for road carriages had a habit of overturning. But

Most of the early railroad promoters knew exactly what they wanted to carry. They knew what traffic was being carried by water and road, and figured that a railway would do it better. Sometimes they saw a potential asset, like a coal deposit, needing only a railroad track to bring it into the market. Very often, their lines were overwhelmed with traffic they had not expected. Rail lines built in anticipation of passengers quickly found themselves short of capacity for a growing freight demand, and vice versa. This was because so many opportunities presented by each of the railways were unnoticed until a line was actually built, at which point various enterprising citizens grasped their chance. Far from simply meeting existing demands, the railroads were creating entirely new ones. Places of great economic potential, lacking only a means of transportation, suddenly became places of great economic opportunity. Small manufacturers went after the big new market, and their traveling salesmen (or "commercial travellers" in Britain) added to the demand for passenger services even more. Small farmers became prosperous suppliers of distant markets. A hitherto local wine like Chianti could expand its market all over Europe. Growers in Cornwall could supply fresh-cut flowers for London, 250 miles away, and those in Florida could market their fruit in prosperous cities like New York. In due course, this "multiplier effect" became common knowledge, and railways were built in expectation of the traffic that they themselves would stimulate.

The settlement of the American and Canadian West, as well as of Argentina, was not as spontaneous as it may have seemed. Governments contributed to it by encouraging the railway builders through such incentives as land grants. The Illinois Central provides the textbook example of the land-grant railroad, but it was far from being alone. The land grant gave railway builders the financial security they needed and was also a way of attracting immigrants. In due course those immigrants would send the produce from their farmsteads to the cities, and the freight cars would have return loads such as fertilizers, building materials, and high-value merchandise. There was a

whiff of the planned economy in some of these U.S. ventures, even more so in the Canadian Pacific, and one of the later transcontinentals, the Trans Siberian, was an outright government enterprise. It was planned in meticulous detail to satisfy the demands of overpopulation in Old Russia and underpopulation in Siberia, the requirements of imperial strategy, and the growth of Russia's agricultural exports. It was not long before a new brand of produce, Siberian butter, was being sold in London and Paris.

As with work, so with leisure. The claim that the railroads brought more free time is not easy to sustain, although it is true that the alarm caused by accidents due to overtired railway workers was one of the impulses behind laws limiting working hours. What the railways essentially did was make leisure more obvious. Cities and towns extended their fields of gravitation, as steam trains provided the opportunity for day trips into town. The theatre trip and the shopping trip became feasible for people living fifty miles from the city. By swelling the clientele, the railways encouraged the opening of new theatres and new shops, thereby enhancing the city's attraction.

Below: "USSR—A Great Railroad Power," is the message of this Soviet government poster. It dates from the early 1950s, when the steam locomotive was still regarded as part of the Russian future.

The cities grew, and their residents needed fresh air. Railway-served residential settlements outside town—suburbs—appeared, and so did country and seaside resorts at attractive locations within a few hours' train journey of the big city. The excursion business emerged, organized either by the railways themselves or by outsiders, of whom Thomas Cook of Leicester, England, was the most prominent. The excursion train organized by agents was essentially an entire prebooked train, outside the public timetables. With revenue guaranteed, the railway faced a risk-free proposition and was willing to quote a low fare. In Britain the day excursion was a great success and an enormous social benefit, and was soon supplemented by the weekend break. The idea spread very slowly in continental Europe, where distances were greater and populations poorer. But in America the excursion had some appeal, often in the form of longer trips; the train that came to grief on a burning bridge near Chatsworth in 1887 was a sleeping-car excursion from Peoria, Illinois, up to the distant Niagara Falls, New York. In the United States, as elsewhere, the short, closely focused excursion also existed, mostly taking the form of shopping and theatre trips. In Australia, as late as 1971, the busy weekly steam-hauled "Cowra Shoppers Train" was still transporting shoppers from big village to small town.

Another leisure activity that owed its expansion to the railways was organized sport. On British station platforms the wicker homing-pigeon crate was an everyday object. Delivered by passenger train, it awaited the prearranged time when its occupants would be released by station staff to fly home and maybe win a prize in a pigeon-fancy competition—then a popular British sport. Horseboxes were frequently seen, attached to passenger trains. In Britain they were four-wheeled vehicles providing a large stable and a small compartment for the attendant. They transformed horse racing, with prime horses transported by rail from one racecourse to another, thereby converting local meets into national events, while prime "stud" stallions were taken by train from one mare to another. In Australia racing greyhounds were a prominent cargo. In New South Wales at least, there were greyhound passenger coaches. These were suburban vehicles with one side of each carriage converted to individual kennels, the seats on the other side being

Below: Competition in North America: for many miles outside Montreal, the Canadian Pacific trains (background) ran alongside the competing Canadian National line (foreground). The picture dates from the 1950s and shows a Canadian Pacific Montreal-Ottawa train.

left for the attendants. That way, the dogs could travel as "honorary humans." British railways also carried dogs, and there was a long court case during the mid-nineteenth century after one coursing champion, carelessly resting his tail on the station platform, had it run over by a trolley. The owner eventually collected twenty-five pounds as compensation.

Later, in many countries, the railway enabled soccer and other sports teams to play anywhere, so national championships could be organized. The "football special," the low-price excursion train taking soccer supporters to away matches, became commonplace. These supporters were not ideal passengers, and there was some vandalism, but this was outweighed by the financial gain of finding traffic for passenger trains that would otherwise be idle on weekends. In the United States, where distances were far greater, the pattern was not quite the same, but the college-football special, sometimes split into a half-dozen heavily loaded trains, was a regular event for some cities.

The steam railway was pre-eminently a carrier of bulk commodities, thriving on volume. This meant that some communities were unable to attract railway promoters. Occasionally, even a city was bypassed by the railways, Novgorod in Russia being a prime example of how a great city could decline if denied the new form of transportation. Some relief from this situation was thought to be offered by the narrow-gauge railway, which was much cheaper to build. In British India, a meter-gauge network was built to feed the broad-gauge main lines. In France, too, meter-gauge systems appeared. Elsewhere in continental Europe, the 750mm (2ft 6in) gauge became popular. In the United States, the 3ft gauge

appeared (and survives on tourist lines in Colorado). It was also used on some South American lines engineered by Americans. The narrow gauge was ideal for mountainous terrain, as it made sharp curves possible, and it brought prosperity to many settlements throughout the world. But it was rarely very profitable, and the arrival of the motor bus and motor truck in the twentieth century put an end to its further development and led, eventually, to the closure of many lines.

There were also broad gauges, which had technical advantages over the "Stephenson" gauge of 4ft 8-1/2in. Britain's 7ft 1/4in gauge of the Great Western, while obviously superior, succumbed to the demands of gauge standardization, but in Spain and India the 5ft 6in gauge flourished and became "standard." The abandonment of the broad gauge in Britain was a case of the triumph of the second-best, in the sense that the Stephenson gauge prevailed because it got in first. In Britain, as well, the longer-established vacuum brake

Above: *An Australian racing dog awaits his train on a station platform in New South Wales.*

triumphed over the higher-performance air brake. The conflict between standard gauge and broad gauge foreshadowed the electronic age in which aggressively marketed second-rate solutions would again overwhelm superior rivals.

As railway companies emerged, they had to develop organizational structures, with managing hierarchies, chains of command, and ways of supervising workers who might be hundreds of miles away from their company base. In the very early days of British railways, many managers were, in fact, retired army officers, so a military pattern, with its discipline and regularity, was adopted. This rigidity was matched or exceeded in other countries. In Prussia, railway staff were required to stand smartly at attention as trains passed. This practice was imitated, less smartly, in some neighboring countries. In Russia, even after the steam age, it was customary for staff to go through the military motion of presenting arms, using their flag or staff in place of a rifle. This ritual signified that all was in order. Strict discipline and a fixed chain of command were suited to a technology that was complex and worked

by timetable, but this rigidity became a handicap when the railroads faced more flexible competitors in the form of highway operators.

Yet in the first major war, whose course was determined by railway potentials, militarization of railroads failed. This was the American Civil War, in which the North had an advantage in its rail potential and made good use of it to dispatch troops in unexpected directions at unexpected speeds. The South was handicapped not only by its relative lack of railroad engineering potential, but in its imposition of strict military control on its lines. With military officers in command, movement tended to come to a standstill. One factor the military mind could not seem to grasp was that rolling stock has to be returned after unloading; freight cars could not be used as stationary warehouses at their destination or hoarded in case of need. The North had the wisdom to leave railroad managers in charge, bestowing military rank on them to ensure that their orders were observed, and its trains ran well.

In continental Europe, the railway enabled the creation of new mass armies

Below: A German World War II "Kriegslok" locomotive. This unit was photographed in the 1960s, having become part of the Austrian Railways locomotive stock.

based on conscription. Calling up entire age groups year by year, training them over a short period of service, and then sending them back to civilian life as reservists to be promptly called back in case of war, depended upon rail transportation. General staffs had entire departments devoted to scheduling the intricate details by which units would be assembled from reservists and sent with the right equipment to the right sector of the frontier at precisely the right time. These procedures failed in the Russo-Japanese War of 1904–05, the Japanese having deliberately started the war before the Trans Siberian Railway was anywhere near its full capacity. Unable to move its huge army to the Far East, big Russia was beaten by small Japan. War by timetable reached its peak in World War I. It was said later that the war came because there was no scope for last-minute diplomacy; once set into motion, the military timetables had to take their ordained course. This was not actually true, but as at least one general staff believed it, it became self-fulfilling.

Railways also had a part to play at the front line, and so-called trench railways appeared. These were to supply the trenches with men and ammunition, and they used narrow-gauge tracks that could be easily relaid as the front moved. Most armies had stocks of locomotives, but these were soon overwhelmed by the sheer scale of World War I, so U.S.-built trench locomotives were imported in large numbers. Armies also ran their own full-sized supply trains behind the frontiers, borrowing locomotives from the railway companies at first, but eventually ordering their own locomotive types. The U.S. "Pershing" locomotives that worked in France between the wars

had been built to move American troops and supplies from the French Atlantic ports to the Western Front. During World War II, Great Britain, the United States, and Germany all mass-produced "war locomotives" designed to manage the traffic in newly won territories, as well as to ease locomotive shortages elsewhere. Of these, the German *Kriegslok* ("war loco") was exceptional both in its quantity (about 6,000 were built) and its technology (it was progressively downgraded so that it consumed the cheapest metals and could be built by unskilled slave labor). Curiously, despite its downgrading, it proved to be a very long-lasting design. One unit remained in regular service in Poland into the twenty-first century.

Above: One of the hundreds of U.S. Transportation Corps locomotives built for service in Europe after the Allied invasion. This unit was retained by the British army engineers' Longmoor Military Railway.

Below: The equivalent British war-service locomotive, the "Austerity" design, built for the British army but acquired by several countries after the end of World War II.

Early Locomotives

It took a century for the steam locomotive to develop fully, the final major step forward being the fitting of superheaters from about 1900 onward. After that, there were some improvements in drafting, but nothing fundamental. Locomotive development was not so much a process of invention as of solution; problems were realized and solved largely by informed trial and error. It was a case of innovation waiting to happen as the development process continued. Only Richard Trevithick, who produced the first recognizable steam railway locomotive in 1804, was a true innovator who owed little to the work of predecessors. He died poor.

Trevithick's locomotive in South Wales, although it damaged the track, showed what could be done and, with horse power expensive because of the Napoleonic Wars, steam locomotives were built for colliery (coal mine) lines in northeastern England. The now-preserved *Puffing Billy* was one of four locomotives that in 1813 replaced fifty horses. It was the creation of the Wylam Colliery manager, William Hedley. The hard-to-believe idea that a smooth wheel could exert traction power on a smooth rail without slipping was finally accepted at this point. (It might have been thought that Trevithick's venture had proved this a decade earlier, but that locomotive hauled only 25 tons). In 1812 a successful colliery railway had a "rack" of cog teeth laid alongside the track, to be engaged by a steam-turned cog-wheel on the locomotive. This was the Middleton Railway, and its founder, John Blenkinsop, though wrong in his initial supposition, paved the way for future rack railways that were used on steep mountain alignments.

George Stephenson, who grew up in this area of steam activity, copied the Middleton locomotives but left out the cog arrangement. To increase wheel-to-rail adhesion he at one point had a chain drive spreading the power to the tender wheels, but this proved unnecessary. This, his first locomotive, was called *Blucher*, and was one of the landmark designs that Stephenson and his son Robert produced over the next two decades. Stephenson built several successors to *Blucher* for colliery work and in 1825 produced *Locomotion* for the Stockton & Darlington Railway, a public railway that used steam power as well as horses. *Locomotion's* innovation was the use of outside coupling rods, which shared the turning power among all four wheels.

The Stephensons' next landmark locomotive was *Rocket*, their entry in the "Rainhill trials" of 1829. These trials were staged by the Liverpool & Manchester Railway, then under construction, on the

Opposite: The De Witt Clinton, *built by the West Point Foundry in 1831 for the Mohawk and Hudson RR. It could haul up to 8 tons at 30 mph. This is an authentic replica built for the 1893 Chicago World's Fair.*

Above: One of Edward Bury's locomotives. This example, now preserved at Britain's National Railway Museum, was built for the Furness Railway, but many were exported and influenced U.S. locomotive design. They had bar frames and a tall copper firebox.

advice of George Stephenson. Other entries in the trials included a vertical boiler machine designed by Ericsson. This, *Novelty*, broke down in the trials and its inventor went to the United States where, decades later, he would be more successful with his *Monitor* ironclad, designed for the Union Navy. Another competitor was Timothy Hackworth, who was associated with the Stephensons on the Stockton & Darlington Railway and who had developed the blastpipe concept, in which exhaust steam passes up the chimney to create a draft for the fire, making a self-regulating system in which the harder the engine works, the hotter the fire becomes. *Rocket* incorporated a blastpipe feature and also had a multitubular boiler, in which the hot gas from the fire passes through tubes immersed in the boiler before exhausting to chimney. This

idea, which was not invented by the Stephensons, made much more effective use of the heat released by the fuel. Perhaps most significantly, *Rocket* incorporated the Stephensons' direct drive from cylinders to wheels by means of connecting rods acting on offset pins (crankpins) set in the wheels. *Rocket* performed spectacularly at the trials, pulling its load reliably and reaching what at the time was the fantastic speed of 30 miles per hour. But while perseverance, talent, and luck advanced the Stephensons, they were not the only steam locomotive pioneers. Hackworth made several contributions, and in France Marc Seguin did likewise.

Although the United States had imported pre-*Rocket*-type locomotives from England, including *Stourbridge Lion* and three others for the Delaware & Hudson RR (which found them unsuited

Left: *A 1926 replica of the vertical-boiler Tom Thumb, originally built by a New York engineer in 1829. Although it ran out of steam in its race against a horse, this locomotive persuaded the Baltimore & Ohio RR to use steam power.*

for its tracks), as early as 1830 the West Point Foundry built the *Best Friend of Charleston* for the South Carolina Railroad. That railroad was the first American public line to operate steam locomotives on a regular basis. The locomotive itself was best known for a boiler explosion, caused by its fireman's interference with the safety valve. Although in the 1830s the United States imported about 100 locomotives from England, this reflected lack of manufacturing capacity rather than of technical expertise. Indeed, as early as 1832 John Jervis designed for the Mohawk & Hudson RR his *Experiment*, notable for its leading four-wheel truck.

Many of the English locomotives supplied to U.S. railroads were of the Bury type. Edward Bury, locomotive superintendent of the London & Birmingham Railway from the late 1830s, had earlier devised his own concept of the steam locomotive. It was characterized by the big domed firebox (forerunner of the domed boiler) and bar frames. It used

inside cylinders that acted on a cranked driving axle. Bar frames became standard on subsequent U.S. locomotives, whereas the British preferred plate frames throughout the steam era. Bar frames were simpler to build—a blacksmith could do it—and allowed easier access to internal mechanisms. Plate frames were

Below: Probably the oldest steam locomotive still operable, Lion is an early example of the 0-4-2 wheel arrangement, and was built for the Liverpool & Manchester Railway in 1838.

Above: A Crampton patent locomotive, in which the driving axle was behind the firebox, making more space for the latter. Such locomotives were fast and steady and became popular in continental Europe, though this example was built in 1848 for a Scottish railway. This is one of the earliest locomotive photographs, taken in about 1850.

stronger in some ways; they were harder to repair but less likely to need repair.

The Bury four-wheeler (having a 0-4-0 wheel arrangement) was a successful model and one early American locomotive company, that of the Norris brothers, developed it by replacing the leading axle with a four-wheel leading truck, making a 4-2-0 wheel arrangement. The Bury-type firebox overhung the rear, and the cylinders were outside, providing better access and to some extent keeping them cool. This Norris 4-2-0 became a standard, almost traditional, American model. Some were even exported to Britain, where the Birmingham & Gloucester Railway ordered a batch, one of which suffered a lethal boiler explosion. It was not long before the Norris 4-2-0 was given an extra pair of driving wheels, located behind the firebox, thus creating the 4-4-0 wheel arrangement, which was known as the "American Type"—aptly so, because in an improved form the outside-cylinder 4-4-0 dominated U.S. railroads for several decades.

Meanwhile the Stephensons had produced their *Planet* model. This had inside cylinders and an extra axle behind the firebox. Unlike the bar-framed *Rocket*, these locomotives had plate frames. The

Planets trains marked the parting of the ways for British and American design concepts; their plate frames and short wheelbase were suited to finely engineered British lines but were very unsuitable for the United States. Those that were imported by American railroads were soon rebuilt, the *John Bull* of the Camden & Amboy RR being fitted with a leading truck and pilot (or "cowcatcher"). The shortcomings of the Stephenson design gave Norris engines a ready market.

From the *Planet* was derived the Stephensons' *Patentee*. This 2-2-2 had double framing (the wheels being sandwiched between inside and outside plates), an arrangement that was favored for several decades in Britain. *Patentee* was the origin of the "single" locomotive favored by British companies for fast trains in the nineteenth century. The "single" had one pair of very large driving wheels, enabling it to reach high speeds without overheating. Originally a 2-2-2, it became a 4-2-2 when a leading truck was provided for the sake of stability at high speed. It went out of fashion when heavier trains made it liable to wheelslip, but had a fresh lease of life at the end of the century when steam sanding gear was developed. It was very much a British concept. In the United States it had little use.

Later, the *Patentee* provided the foundation for the 2-4-0 type, in which a coupled pair of axles replaced the "single" driving axle, a response to the wheelslip problem. It was also the origin of that British favorite, the six-wheeler. The latter was one of the Stephenson "long-boiler" family, in which the firebox was placed behind the rearmost wheels, allowing a longer boiler to be carried. The 2-4-0 was also a long-boiler type and was developed, notably in France, to a 2-4-2 wheel arrangement. In Britain, right up to the end of the steam age, the inside-cylinder six-wheeler (0-6-0) was a mainstay of both freight and secondary passenger work. In America the six-wheeler was confined to yard work because of the stability problems associated with the short wheelbase and long overhang. The British railways would eventually design six-wheelers with a longer wheelbase.

In America, whereas in the early 1840s two-thirds of the locomotives were of the 4-2-0 type, by 1870 four-fifths were of the 4-4-0 wheel arrangement. Early 4-4-0 examples had been rather rigid developments of the *Patentee*, but American mechanics soon applied equalized suspension of the driving wheels, providing a smooth ride over rough track. These engines were used for both passenger and freight work and apart from some early

examples they had outside cylinders. At mid-century, when the cylinders had come down to a horizontal alignment, the leading truck was lengthened to make space for them. Provision of a bigger "wagon-top" firebox meant that the boiler was sharply tapered at the rear. In Britain the 4-4-0 was a purely passenger engine and had inside cylinders.

Later in the nineteenth century, when freight trains became heavier, the 2-6-0 wheel arrangement was tried, soon to be succeeded by the 2-8-0, which also became very prevalent in the United States. The 2-6-0 continued to exist as a general-purpose secondary line locomotive, and the 4-6-0 appeared as a more powerful development of the 4-4-0. The 4-6-0, or "ten-wheeler," was a useful engine but never attained in the United States the popularity it won in Britain and parts of continental Europe. It was soon replaced on top passenger duties by

Below: Despite its identification as Canadian Pacific No 1, this American 4-4-0 was not the first locomotive built for that railway. It was acquired second-hand, and was originally built in Philadelphia for the Northern Pacific RR in 1872.

Above: *This 4-4-0 design was introduced by Austria's Südbahn in 1885 for hauling international trains from Vienna. It is double-framed and has two steam domes, each with a different type of safety valve. Running on light track over a twisting and heavily graded alignment, Austrian locomotives had distinctive design features.*

the 4-6-2, or Pacific. This, like its less popular predecessor the 4-4-2 or Atlantic, had a rear carrying truck to bear the weight of a big firebox, the size of firebox being a main determinant of the horsepower output of a locomotive. In Britain, and most of Europe, the introduction of the new wheel arrangements followed the North American examples with a time lag of a decade or so. The 4-6-0 and 4-6-2 remained the main passenger type in Britain until the end of steam, and this was largely true of the other European countries. The wheel arrangements of the larger American twentieth-century locomotives were rarely adopted by European railways, although Russia had its 2-10-2s and 2-8-4s, and France had some 4-8-2s, while the 4-8-4, an American classic, was also used by Spanish railway carriers.

Fundamental technical advances that determined the subsequent form of the steam locomotive included the brick arch in the firebox, developed during the 1850s. This forced the smoke and gas to take a longer route over the top of the fire, where it combusted further, both cleaning the smoke and producing more heat energy. This made it feasible to burn coal. Hitherto in Britain and Europe the more expensive coke had been used. In America, wood fuel prevailed during this period, but it would soon be superseded by coal.

Many forms of valve gear (the arrangement of rods, shafts, and links that enabled steam to be admitted and released from the cylinders at the moments appropriate for the given mode of operation) were devised in the nineteenth century. The form that eventually became the most popular was invented simultaneously by a Belgian and a Prussian (which is why the Walschaerts valve gear was called the Heusinger valve gear in Germany).

The French balloonist Henri Giffard invented the injector in the 1850s, which forced feedwater into the boiler without the use of pumps. It was very ingenious, exploiting several laws of physics, but had a high failure rate, so most locomotives were fitted with two.

The last fundamental development was the superheater. This was intended to reheat the steam before it entered the cylinders, to avoid the pressure loss and condensation when it cooled prematurely. Many attempts were made at this, most of which worked in prototypes but proved unreliable in the hot, jolting, steam locomotive. It was a Prussian, Wilhelm Schmidt, known to his friends as "Hot-Steam Willy," who ultimately succeeded. He enlarged some of the boiler tubes carrying hot gases from fire to chimney and inserted smaller tubes inside them. These smaller tubes carried the steam on its way to the cylinders, and it was thereby brought to a very high temperature. The fitting of superheaters enhanced locomotive performance, bringing increased output and lower fuel consumption.

Another way of increasing the energy obtained from fuel was compounding, in which steam was first used in high-pressure cylinders and then made to give up more of its expansive energy in low-pressure cylinders. The compound locomotive was developed largely in Prussia and France. Its performance matched expectations, usually, but it was more expensive to build and maintain.

By 1914 the multiplicity of locomotive-building companies had been reduced to a smaller number of large concerns. In America some well-known companies like Norris, Rogers, and Mason that had, in their time, brought considerable innovation to their products had disappeared, leaving three big builders: Baldwin, Lima, and Alco (American Locomotive, an amalgamation of several notable companies). A small number of railroads, notably the Pennsylvania at Altoona, built their own machines. In Britain a similar process was taking place with, for example, the North British Locomotive Company unifying the Glasgow builders. Britain was exceptional in that all its main railway operators designed and built their own locomotives, so the commercial builders relied on the export trade. German builders had both their home railways and exports as a market, and the same applied to French and Belgian builders. Most of these companies introduced successful innovations at some point: Krupp was the first to produce all-steel locomotive wheels (in 1851); French companies were the most succesful pioneers of the compound locomotive; and Lima built the remarkable Shay locomotive for flimsy forestry lines. These and other innovations will be mentioned in the following two chapters.

Below: Old 2-4-2 locomotives of France's Paris-Orleans Railway. Introduced in the 1870s to haul fast trains between Paris and Bordeaux, they lasted on secondary services until the 1950s. They are shown here awaiting their final destination — a scrapyard — in 1954.

Opposite, above: After its 1831 boiler explosion the *Best Friend of Charleston* was reassembled to create this locomotive, *Phoenix*. A significant difference was that in the original design the boiler was placed at the front, which had resulted in poor weight distribution.

Opposite, below: *Invicta*, an early Stephenson locomotive similar to *Rocket*, but with cylinders at the front instead of the rear and with coupled wheels. It was built in 1830 for the Canterbury & Whitstable Railway in southern England. The picture shows it without rods, awaiting restoration.

Above: Small, sometimes one-man, engineering companies tried their hand at steam locomotive construction, often to individualistic designs. In Britain, makers of agricultural machinery built small yard locomotives. This American product is simply constructed and distinctive. The firebox is awkward, but the locomotive has very good visibility.

Left: Britain's Grand Junction Railway introduced the Crewe-type locomotive. This had both inside and outside frames, with the wheels and pistons placed between them, as can be seen in this picture. First produced in the mid-1840s, the type was built up to the late 1850s and was also produced in France.

Below: A side view of the "Crewe" locomotive, now exhibited in Britain's National Railway Museum. This is *Columbine*, built in 1845 for the Grand Junction Railway. Having outside cylinders, the design was an alternative to the Stephenson inside-cylinder layout with its vulnerable cranked driving axle.

Above: Geared steam locomotives were rare, but the English firm of Aveling & Porter, makers of the rather similar steam road-rollers, specialized in them. They had a flywheel as well as geared transmission and could apply a strong tractive effort very smoothly. The picture shows one at work on a British tourist railway.

Above: Displaying the typical characteristics of the American mid-century 4-4-0, No. 25 of the Baltimore & Ohio RR has a big oil lamp, massive spark arrestor, comfortable cab, and sharp taper of the boiler between the two domes (the forward dome is for sand). Use of bar frames gives easy access to the moving parts.

Right: *William Crooks,* one of the fine locomotives built by the short-lived but high-quality New Jersey Locomotive & Machine Company at Paterson. This 4-4-0 is the only locomotive of that company to survive into preservation. Built in 1861 for the St. Paul & Pacific RR (later the Great Northern), it was the first locomotive in Minnesota, and was subsequently placed on exhibition at Duluth.

Opposite, above: This four-wheeler was bought in 1836 for a short line sponsored by the citizens of Natchez, Mississippi, to protect their cotton trade. Financial problems caused the line to sell off first its slaves and then its locomotive in the early 1840s. The line was closed down, but later became part of the Illinois Central.

Opposite, below: *Texas*, one of the first locomotives in that state. Built in 1853, this locomotive won fame, and eventual preservation, for its part in the "Great Locomotive Chase" of the Civil War.

Overleaf: A Glasgow-built 2-4-0 at work in Indonesia. Built in the 1880s, these engines lasted almost a hundred years, mostly working on flimsy branch lines. This example, photographed in 1972, was still a wood burner at this late date.

Below: Illinois Central RR No. 1, built by the Rogers Company in 1852. Made in New Jersey, it was delivered by ship to Chicago. Like its sisters, Engines 2 and 3, it had 5ft driving wheels and weighed about 25 tons.

Above: A British "Single" locomotive of the Great Western Railway. This Railway was built using the broad, 7ft, gauge, so to operate this replica a length of broad-gauge track has been laid at the National Railway Museum. This *Iron Duke* class was designed in the 1840s, and the wrought-iron driving wheels were of 8ft diameter.

Opposite, above: Stephenson's *Locomotion*, as used on the Stockton & Darlington Railway in 1825. This replica shows the vertical cylinder arrangement, which was soon outdated. The original *Locomotion* still exists, but is not operable.

Opposite, below: A U.S. ten-wheeler on exhibition at the Galveston Railroad Museum in Texas.

Below: The original *Rocket* underwent several post-accident repairs and rebuildings before retiring to preservation. This picture shows the boiler riveting. The locomotive was built mainly of iron, but copper was used for the firebox and steam pipes.

National Locomotive Styles

As the decades passed, it became possible to recognize different schools of locomotive design. These distinctions were evident both in fundamentals, like the U.S. preference for bar frames rather than plate frames, or in superficial matters, like the British tendency to hide auxiliary equipment from view. Within a given country, there were also distinctions between the products of individual builders. This was most marked in Britain, where each of the railways had its own locomotive works that developed its own style.

At any given period, American locomotives were larger than those of other countries. This resulted from both need and opportunity: traffic flows were big enough to support heavy trains; manning costs were high enough to make small trains uneconomical; and height and width clearances were generous. Ruggedness and suitability for easy repair without going into a main works were also desirable features in the American locomotive, whereas high thermodynamic efficiency was less important because fuel was abundant.

One of the advantages of bar frames was that they allowed space for large fireboxes. The wide grate became common in North America and enabled low-calorie coal to be used. An extreme development was the Wootten firebox, designed to burn anthracite wastes, which was so big that the cab was mounted on the boiler, "camelback" style. The Wootten firebox never became widespread, but the wide firebox, supported by a pair of carrying wheels, was embodied in the "Atlantic," or 4-4-2, and then the "Pacific," or 4-6-2. The grate of the 4-6-2s became so big that it could not be used to its full capacity without a mechanical stoker. The Pennsylvania Railroad's K4 of 1914 was the world's most powerful Pacific-type locomotive. This was a development of that railroad's E6 4-4-2 of 1910, which distinguished itself in competitive running on the Atlantic City line.

In Britain the wide firebox appeared on the so-called "Ivatt Atlantics" of the

Opposite: A "Midland Compound" leaves Carlisle, northern England. Compounding was rare in Britain, but the parallel boiler and square Belpaire firebox were favored by most railways.

Below: One of the London Brighton and South Coast Railway's Atlantics, a design copied from the Great Northern Railway Atlantic, with its wide round-top firebox.

Great Northern Railway, used on the East Coast main line and of indifferent performance until superheaters were fitted, after which they were outstanding locomotives. The wide firebox was repeated in subsequent Pacific locomotives, including the celebrated *Flying Scotsman*-type and its successor, the A4 streamlined Pacifics, which included the record-breaking *Mallard*. However, the narrow, rather long, firebox was most often used in Britain.

In America enlargement of the Pacific took two routes. The trailing two-wheel truck was replaced by a four-wheel truck to create the 4-6-4 ("Hudson") wheel arrangement with an extra-large firebox; effectively, this produced a Pacific engine with an increased horsepower output. Alternatively, an extra pair of driving wheels was provided, creating a 4-8-2, or "Mountain," which had greater tractive force. These two models soon converged in the 4-8-4, or "Northern," which became a classic American locomotive for passenger and fast-freight work.

The U.S. railroads were not big users of tank locomotives. Such locomotives carried fuel and water on their own frames and, because they dispensed with a tender, did not need turning at the end of their runs. Britain, France, and Germany, with their large urban conglomerations, were great users of tank locomotives for commuter services, the designs of which were simply modifications of existing tender-locomotive designs. Thus the 4-4-0 tender locomotive became a 4-4-2 in its tank-engine version, the extra axle carrying the coal bunker. In Britain the 2-6-2 eventually became the most popular wheel arrangement for tank locomotives, but some railways built bigger types. The Brighton Line used big tank locomotives for its fast intercity, short-distance trains between London and Brighton, while the later LMS Railway built some very competent 2-6-4 tank engines for fast outer-suburban trains. In America the six-wheel tank locomotive was used for yard work in industry, and there was a specifically American commuter tank locomotive, the "Forney Tank," which carried its water, not in side tanks as in Europe, but in a tank located behind the cab.

For freight haulage, the U.S. railroads replaced the "Consolidation," or 2-8-0, with the 2-8-2 ("Mikado") and 2-10-0. The 2-10-0 was also adopted for heavy freight work by the French, German, and Russian railroads, and finally, the British. It was not particularly popular in the United States because it was uncomfortable at higher speeds; its successor, the 2-10-2, was little better in this respect. However, the British examples, built in the final days of steam, appeared to overcome this deficiency and sometimes were even used on fast passenger trains. As for the Mikado, this was immediately popular and was widely used in North America

Below: A P8 ten-wheeler of Prussian Railways. This class was found in Germany and Central Europe, becoming the world's most numerous passenger-locomotive design. Like other types of the Prussian school, it was designed for reliability rather than for brilliant performance.

for all kinds of traffic. It was not favored in Britain, probably for reasons of technical conservatism, but was used in France and Germany. The French design, the 141P, proved to be one of the world's most effective locomotive designs in terms of power for weight. Fresh locomotives of this wheel arrangement, the 141R class, were imported from the United States and Canada for the rehabilitation of French railways after World War II. They brought American design features to a country that had developed its own unique school of locomotive design, but the new adaptation settled down well.

French locomotive designers made their mark with the compound locomotive. What became known as the Nord compounds made their first appearance in the 1890s, and were evolved up to the end of steam after World War II. They had two high-pressure cylinders outside and two low-pressure cylinders inside the frames, with each pair driving different axles. The Nord Atlantic of 1899 developed from the Nord 4-4-0, and was itself the origin of the Nord 4-6-0. Later, the Nord and other French railways used compound Pacific locomotives, as well as 2-8-2 and 4-8-2 variants. Such locomotives cost more to build and maintain, and required competent and devoted crews, but using their steam twice over, they needed less fuel and water and also had a more even pull and rode better. Power for weight was higher and acceleration was faster. Some of these advantages were reduced when superheaters were fitted to noncompound locomotives, but a superheated compound locomotive was unbeatable in terms of energy efficiency.

Compounding did not make a big mark in Britain, where simplicity was the guiding star. The London & North Western

wasted a good deal of money on unsuccessful compound experiments, but the Midland Railway built a compound 4-4-0 that was well liked. This, the "Midland Compound," had three cylinders (two high-pressure outside and one low-pressure inside) and was good enough to be built not only by the MR, but also by its successor, the London Midland & Scottish Railway. The German railways also built compound locomotives of various permutations and in the late nineteenth century relied heavily on the two-cylinder compound. This had one small high-pressure cylinder on one side and a bigger low-pressure cylinder on the other. In terms of efficiency this was a good arrangement, but it was impossible to design such a locomotive with equal power output in both cylinders at all speeds. Therefore, these locomotives tended to yaw alarmingly at higher speeds and were usually confined to low-speed work. The idea was also popular in Russia, at that time a close follower of German practice.

In North America compounding made little headway, although the Baldwin Works did produce the new "Vauclain

Above: One of the hundreds of QJ type freight locomotives still at work in China on heavy freight haulage, sometimes operating in pairs. The design was strongly influenced by Russian practice.

Below: Only sixty years separate Southern Pacific No 1, shipped from its New Jersey builders to California via Cape Horn, and the massive 2-10-2 built during World War I for the SP. Despite the size difference, they are both unmistakably American, with their bar frames, pilots ("cow-catchers"), powerful headlamps, and cab front doors.

Compound," in which the high-pressure and low-pressure cylinders were situated one above the other on each side, each pair driving through the same connecting rod. The model worked well enough, but it was not particularly well-suited to American conditions. However, compounding did enter American practice by a different route — the "Mallet" articulated (flexible-wheelbase) locomotive.

Many articulated locomotives were devised, and a few of these met with success. The challenge they addressed was the conflict between increased haulage power, which demanded more coupled driving wheels, and the limited ability of the large wheelbase formed by those coupled wheels in handling curves. The objective was to find a way of breaking up the coupled wheels into two independent blocks that could rotate to some extent. The Mallet concept, developed by

a Franco-Swiss engineer, had two power trucks of coupled wheels, each with its own set of cylinders. The leading set was pivoted, giving the required flexibility on curves. The main problem was designing flexible joints in the pipes taking steam to the pivoting power unit. This was facilitated by making the locomotive a compound, so it was the once-used steam that was piped to the pivoted truck; the lower-pressure steam was less likely to leak.

The Mallet locomotives were originally small machines intended for narrow-gauge, heavily curved mountain lines, in which role they became quite popular, especially in France and Germany. In America the Baltimore & Ohio adopted the idea for a powerful one-off pusher locomotive, which was so successful that it was followed by numerous classes of heavy-duty Mallet locomotives for freight work. Eventually these became so big that

the low-pressure cylinders were 4 feet in diameter. Beyond this, even the American width limitations became an obstacle, so the compound idea (and hence large low-pressure cylinders) was abandoned for the largest types. Two of the latter, the Chesapeake & Ohio's 2-6-6-6 and the Union Pacific's "Big Boy" 4-8-8-4, were destined to remain the world's biggest-ever steam locomotive types.

The unusual six-wheel rear truck of the C&O Mallet was used to support a massive firebox. All the big U.S. locomotives were provided with a mechanical stoker, because their fireboxes were too large to be served by a man with a shovel. In 1938 the Interstate Commerce Commission ruled that coal-burning engines weighing more than 160,000 lbs (passenger) or 175,000 lbs (freight) on driving wheels should have a mechanical stoker.

During the 1920s the four-wheel truck had become popular for the so-called super-power generation of U.S. designs. The first of these had the then-unusual wheel arrangement of 2-8-4, which was subsequently imitated by the Russians for their *Iosif Stalin*-type passenger locomotives.

Two flexible-wheelbase concepts originated in Britain. The Fairlie locomotive had two boilers back-to-back with the cab in the center, with a pivoted powered truck at each end. It was bought for a few narrow-gauge lines and proved quite successful. In Russia it was also used on the broad gauge in the Caucasian Mountains. The other British flexible-wheelbase innovation was embodied in the Garratt. This had two powered engine units that also carried the coal and water. Slung between these units were the boiler and cab. This was a highly successful idea. Apart from spreading the weight and providing a flexible wheelbase, there was a gap below the

boiler that enabled a deep and well-drafted firebox to be fitted. Although it was not very popular in Britain itself, the Garratt was widely used in the British Commonwealth (especially in Africa, but not in Canada). The South African railways carried out comparative tests of Garratt and Mallet designs and found that the Garratt was clearly superior. But it was not adopted in America, whose railroads remained satisfied with the Mallet.

The United States originated and was the main user of another flexible-wheel-

Above: A lightweight 4-8-4 built for Mexican National Railways in 1946, one of a class of thirty-two.

Below: A Baltimore & Ohio RR "Camelback," in which the engineer rode in relative comfort while the fireman labored on the footplate, shoveling anthracite.

Above: Many narrow-gauge sugar-cane railways on Pacific and Caribbean islands used U.S.-built locomotives. In Hawaii this tourist passenger service is operated on Maui Island.

Opposite, above: A 424 class 4-8-0, the peak of Hungarian locomotive design.

Opposite, below: Union Pacific No 618 now hauls passenger trains on the Heber Valley RR in Utah, but was one of more than 450 2-8-0 freight locomotives built for the UP in the first decade of the twentieth century.

base type, the Shay locomotive, which was introduced in the 1870s. It was intended for the curved, flimsy tracks of lumber companies and ran on pivoted trucks powered by a flexible arrangement of shafts and gears rotated by vertical cylinders placed on one side of the boiler, which was fixed off-center. This design was built in large numbers by the Lima Locomotive Works. Competitors in the form of the Heisler and Climax locomotives soon appeared, but were never quite as successful as the Shay.

Apart from the Garratt and Fairlie, British locomotive development produced few significant innovations. The trend was simply to move forward from one design to another, hoping to incorporate small improvements. When the time came to replace the long-lived 4-4-0 with something more powerful, enlargement to the 4-4-2 or 4-6-0 types was not as straightforward as expected, and a number of mediocre designs were produced. George

Churchward, of the Great Western, who was reviewing the entire situation, decided to make a fresh start. Studying American practice, and importing a handful of French compounds, he achieved the rare feat of imitating the best foreign practice while preserving what was good of the British tradition. His locomotives had the tapered American-style boiler, supported on a saddle to which outside cylinders were bolted. Trials with the French compounds had suggested that they were only marginally superior to the well-designed noncompound, but many of their features were found to be worth imitating, particularly the layout of their four cylinders. For his big passenger engine, the *Star* series, Churchward did employ four cylinders. He also paid attention to the pipes, valves, and chambers through which the steam passed on its way to the cylinders. By easing the passage of the steam, a new level of efficiency was obtained. Although he did build one Pacific, Churchward preferred the 4-6-0, and the GWR stayed with that wheel arrangement, using the two-cylinder 2-8-0 and 2-6-0 types for other services and a range of 2-6-2 tank types for suburban work. Notably among British designers, Churchward did not produce an 0-6-0, a popular wheel arrangement in Britain but less than ideal in terms of riding qualities.

Churchward's ideas slowly, very slowly, spread to the other British companies, and it was not until the 1940s that a fresh wave of innovation occurred, when Oliver Bulleid introduced controversial designs to the Southern Railway. His three-cylinder "air-smoothed" Pacifics were built in large numbers and incorporated such innovations as chain-driven valve gear and attention to the crew's comfort. They performed very well, but needed very careful maintenance, so they were not favored by Bulleid's successors. Instead, the newly nationalized British Railways introduced a range of locomotives based on those of the former London Midland & Scottish Railway, which themselves were derived from pre-1914 Great Western innovations.

In a role corresponding to Churchward's in Britain was André Chapelon of France, usually rated as the foremost twentieth-century steam-locomotive engineer. His specialty was adapting designs whose performance had never matched their potential and improving, even transforming, them. This he did with such devices as better steam passages, hotter superheating, and smoother exhausts by means of double chimneys. In one notable example, he doubled the horsepower output of a design. The "Chapelon Pacific" became a classic. It existed in several varieties, depending upon which original design had been utilized. In the 1940s Chapelon and others were experimenting with advanced 4-6-4 and 4-8-4 designs, but electrification put an end to these. Other Chapelon locomotives included a six-cylinder 2-12-0 compound prototype, a series of 4-8-2 compounds (241P class), and fast 4-8-0 engines for hilly lines.

The major states of Germany had their own locomotive policies until World War I, although Prussia dominated. Bavarian State Railways had some notable bar-frame four-cylinder compound Pacifics, and the Württemberg Railway used compound 2-12-0 locomotives. Prussia had produced some good compound designs, but its most widespread classes, the P8 passenger ten-wheeler and the eight-wheel and ten-wheel freight engines, were noncompound. Prussian policies were embodied in the standard locomotive range developed for the new unified

German state railways (DR) after World War I and were notable for the priority given to reliability and easy maintenance. High boiler pressures were not favored for this reason, and locomotive power-weight ratios were not given great importance. Thus the performance of German standard designs was only moderate, but German locomotives were easy to maintain and slow to break down. The culmination of this conservative design policy was the World War II *Kriegslok* 2-10-0, whose simple construction and high reliability made it ideal for war service.

Austria-Hungary was another state with distinctive locomotives. Having relatively light track and a high proportion of winding, steep-grade main lines, it needed specialized designs. The inspirational engineer there was Karl Golsdorf, whose locomotives had thin frames, low boiler pressures (so boilers could be light), and no running plates or wheel splashers,

again to save weight. Golsdorf preferred two- and four-cylinder compounds and adopted some unusual wheel arrangements, including the 2-6-4. After World War I, Austria and Hungary went their separate ways, Austria producing nothing novel, but Hungary building a range of distinctive locomotives of which one, the Type 424 4-8-0, was outstanding and found service in other countries. Another part of the former Austrian Empire, Czechoslovakia, also produced a distinctive locomotive style and in the post-1945 period designed some outstanding locomotives, including some with French features but without compounding.

Railways of the British Empire relied mainly on British designs at first. Canada, after importing some British locomotives initially, soon turned to American models, some of which were manufactured in Canada by both independent and railroad workshops. After World War I, both the

Below: British-built Garratt locomotives in South Africa. With their sixteen driving wheels, divided into two pivoted power units, these locomotives combined great tractive power with ability to negotiate sharp curves. Some Garratts are still at work in southern Africa.

Canadian Pacific and Canadian National stayed with American concepts but strove to impart some originality to their locomotives by attention to detail.

Australian state railways used British-built locomotives at first. New South Wales relied heavily on the Beyer Peacock Company of Manchester, but there was a tendency for some units of each class to be built in the home state. In the 1940s the distinctive Class 38 Pacific appeared, designed as well as built in New South Wales. This performed well. South Australia, in the interwar period, abruptly changed from British-style to American-style locomotives, but not with resounding effect. Queensland began to build its own locomotives and developed a distinctive family based partly on British and partly on American concepts. Victoria, Tasmania, and Western Australia stayed with the British tradition until the end of the steam age.

South Africa and New Zealand purchased most of their locomotives from British builders, but had their own locomotive departments that specified their particular needs and influenced the ultimate designs. At the very end of the steam age, South African workshops originated a domestic design of yard locomotive. India was a good market for British builders, but after World War II the main passenger locomotive was the WP type, which was designed largely in the United States. Its corresponding freight version, however, seemed to owe more to the British style even while using many of the same components as the WP.

Among Latin American countries, Mexico favored American designs, often buying used locomotives. The last units of two classic American wheel arrangements, the 4-4-0 and 4-8-4, were built for

Mexico. Argentina remained steadily within the British tradition, although some of its locomotives were rebuilt on Chapelon principles. Chile bought locomotives from Britain, Germany, and, eventually, the United States.

In tsarist Russia locomotive design was influenced primarily by Prussian and Austrian practice, as seen in its celebrated ten-wheel freight locomotive, which was destined to be the world's most numerous steam-locomotive type. Under Stalin there was a shift to American practice. A delegation of Soviet engineers visited U.S. locomotive works, was arrested on its return, and put to work designing the American-style FD 2-10-2 and *Iosif Stalin* 2-8-4, both of which were mass-produced for Soviet Railways. However, the last Russian designs produced in series, the P36 4-8-4 and LV 2-10-2, were beginning to show signs of a distinctive Russian school that subsequently influenced the QJ 2-10-2 built for Chinese Railways up to the 1980s, and which is still in service.

Above: Austrian locomotives at night. Both are two-cylinder compounds, with the larger, low-pressure, cylinder facing the camera. The locomotive on the left is a Golsdorf 2-8-0. The double-dome arrangement was a characteristically Austrian feature.

Above: A British V2 2-6-2 locomotive of the London & North Eastern Railway. These locomotives were a scaled-down version of the Great Northern *Flying Scotsman* type and were very successful. With their 74-inch driving wheels they were suited for passenger and fast freight service, and during World War II they dealt successfully with extra-long passenger trains.

Right: This 2-6-0 is from the same design office as the V2 above, and was one of the last designs introduced for the London & North Eastern Railway. Unlike most British locomotives, it had electric lights but, because the position of the portable oil lamps on British locomotives constituted a code indicating the class of train, it carried the old-style lamps as well. This particular locomotive has been preserved and is shown with a regular summer steam service operated in Scotland's Western Highlands.

Opposite, above: An A4 Pacific of the London & North Eastern Railway awaits duty at Grantham, an engine-changing point. The record-breaking *Mallard* was of this three-cylinder class. The nameplate honors one of the company's directors.

Opposite, below: A Churchward "Star" four-cylinder 4-6-0 of the Great Western Railway. This ground-breaking type incorporated American features (including taper boiler and smokebox saddle), and influenced subsequent British designs.

Below: With coal piled dangerously high, a 4-6-2 tank locomotive leaves a Sussex commuter station, bound for London. This locomotive was built by the London Brighton & South Coast Railway, which was one of those companies that used tank locomotives for fast intercity trains (its London-Brighton main line was only 51 miles long).

Left: German steam locomotives are still in regular service on narrow-gauge lines which, though of tourist interest, also serve local populations. Most such lines are in the former German Democratic Republic; 750mm (2ft 6in) and 1,000mm (1 meter, or 3ft 3in) are the most common gauges on these lines.

Below: One of the most powerful narrow-gauge German designs is the meter-gauge 2-10-2 tank engine, some of which were built in the 1930s and others by the Karl Marx Works in 1954. Several are still at work in the Harz Mountain region.

Right: Chapelon's 141P class 2-8-2. This four-cylinder general-purpose locomotive was, in terms of the power/weight ratio, the best of the French compounds.

Opposite, below: After World War II, American builders supplied French Railways with two-cylinder noncompound 2-8-2 locomotives of the 141R class. Two of these very successful locomotives are seen in this photograph at the Calais locomotive depot, flanking a Chapelon compound Pacific.

Below: One of the early "Nord Compounds," introduced in 1897. About 270 of these ten-wheelers were built, and set the style for later French compounds with their small high-pressure cylinders outside and the low-pressure cylinders inside the frame.

Opposite: A Chinese Railways JS class 2-8-2. More than a thousand of these were built from 1958 onward by three Chinese locomotive works. The boiler is of Russian inspiration. They were designed for secondary freight trains, and some are still in use for yard work.

Below: A South African Railways 19D class 2-8-4. This British-built design is characterized by low axle weight and high-capacity tender, being intended for arid branch lines. This particular locomotive is now owned by Rovos Rail of Pretoria, a preservation company.

Opposite, above: Victorian Railways designed and built this K class 2-8-0 at its own workshops. Fifty-three were built between 1919 and 1946. Intended mainly for light freight, they were said to be Australia's most trouble-free locomotives.

Opposite, below: A contrast in Central European tank locomotives. The nearest, a 2-6-2, is a Hungarian design, while the other is an Austrian 2-8-2. Both are shown in service with Yugoslav Railways, which inherited them from the Hapsburg Empire.

Below: A frank imitation of American practice, the Soviet Railways *"Iosif Stalin"* 2-8-4 class was for heavy passenger work. About 600 units were built. Russian railroad specialists visited the United States in 1930, seeking ideas, and later that year many designers were arrested and forced to produce the drawings in captivity.

Above: The Grand Canyon Railway, a steam tourist line, was originally part of the Santa Fe Railway, which developed the tourist potential of the Canyon. The present company uses 2-8-0 locomotives like this, originally built for a Great Lakes iron-ore line.

Opposite: When the Last Spike ceremony signaled completion of the first transcontinental railroad, the Central Pacific RR was represented by the 4-4-0 Engine 60, *Jupiter*. Promontory, Utah, where the ceremony took place, is now preserved as a National Historical Site, with Engine 60 on display.

Above: A Santa Fe RR 4-8-4 locomotive hauling the Chicago-Los Angeles "Grand Canyon" train overtakes a freight train in the Cajon Pass. The locomotive was one of a class of eleven built by Baldwin in 1938, having nickel-steel boilers and 80-inch driving wheels.

Opposite, above: This 4-4-2 was built for the Illinois Central RR in 1903. There were twenty-five in the class, built by Rogers. They had 79-inch driving wheels and weighed 188,000 pounds. Increasing train weights meant that they were superseded by Pacifics within a couple of years.

Left: The Southern Pacific Railroad owned several classes of 4-6-2. This is a unit of the P10 class, built in 1924–25 and having 73-inch driving wheels. They were used on passenger trains until the 1950s.

Previous pages: A Durango & Silverton RR narrow-gauge 2-8-2 at work in Colorado.

Opposite, above: These are American-styled WP class broad-gauge Pacifics, 755 of which were built for Indian Railways, the prototypes being supplied by the Baldwin locomotive works in 1947. Most were built in Canada or in India itself, but there were contributions from Austria and Poland.

Below: A Canadian National 4-6-4 leaves Toronto. This was a small class of five units intended for fast Montreal-Toronto day trains. Built in 1930, they had 80-inch driving wheels. The green-painted valance, the shaping of the chimney, concealment of most piping, and other features were intended to present a specifically Canadian National style.

Opposite, below: A Shay locomotive of Bolivian State Railways. The boiler is offset, making space for the vertical cylinders placed alongside the boiler on the other side. Drive is through rotating rods and bevel gears on the cylinder side.

Fixtures and Fittings

The most seasoned railroad enthusiasts, when presented with a picture of a locomotive, can instantly identify the country, and often the company, of its origin. Identities are sometimes conveyed by superficial signs like the shape of a chimney or the style of the number, but often a family of locomotives can be distinguished by a particular combination of the varied components that might be included or left out of a design.

One readily identifiable component is the firebox, which has "round-top" and "Belpaire" configurations. The Belpaire, named for its Belgian inventor, was square and offered more water space where it counted, above and around the fire. But the round-top was preferred by many engineers because it was cheaper to manufacture. Fashions changed quite easily in this choice, with a change of chief mechanical engineer sometimes prompting a change of boiler type for subsequent designs, and there were many cases of locomotives being rebuilt to accommodate the other type of boiler.

Apart from these two main firebox types, from time to time new variants appeared. These were like so many other innovations in that they often gave the promised results (usually greater thermal efficiency) but at the same time had drawbacks (typically extra maintenance cost).

One device fitted to obtain more heat from the fuel was the feedwater heater. This used some of the exhaust to warm the water that was about to be fed into the boiler. In America the patented Worthington heater was used. This was highly visible, being a cylinder placed crossways on the smokebox in front of the chimney. The feedwater heater was also used in continental Europe. In France, and elsewhere, it took the form of two cylinders placed lengthways behind the chimney. It did have some drawbacks, and it was not used in Britain.

There was a great variety of superheater designs, but most of these were in no way

Opposite: On an American locomotive, the oil headlamp needed to be large enough to illuminate the track ahead. In other countries lights were simply markers, indicating the position of a locomotive.

Below: This American engine has the wheels located between the frames but their crankpins and counterweights outside.

Above: Two meter-gauge Pacifics of Indian Railways shown being dismantled. The superheater has been removed from the smokebox at left, whereas it is still in place on the right-hand locomotive; its elements can be seen bending back inside the boiler tubes.

superior to Wilhelm Schmidt's device, yet sufficiently different to evade the Schmidt patent. Externally, there was no indication of which superheater was fitted. Many locomotives did not have them, because their benefit was felt over long sustained power outputs and they would therefore have been more trouble than they were worth in a yard locomotive. When existing locomotives were modified to include a superheater, a visible sign of the change was a longer smokebox, necessary to accommodate the device.

There was also variety in valve gears. At the dawn of the steam age, changing the positions at which steam entered or left the cylinders was done by an engineman clambering to the valves and making the required adjustment manually. At that time this was important only for changing the direction of movement, but later, when it became uneconomic and self-defeating to admit steam at full pressure for the whole length of the piston stroke, the advantage of changing the entry and cut-off points required a valve gear that would allow regulation from the footplate. The Stephenson

gear was the most popular in the nineteenth century, but in the twentieth it began to lose favor against the Walschaerts gear. There were other patented gear arrangements too, each with their own advantages. No valve gear was perfect over the whole range of speeds. In the United States the Baker gear became common; a variant of the Walschaerts gear and intended originally for traction engines, it was patented in 1903. As for the valves themselves, these were initially flat sliding surfaces, "D-valves," and worked inside square steam chests next to the cylinders. Piston valves, working in cylindrical steam chests, came later and were somewhat more efficient, although requiring greater care in lubrication.

Valve gears could be either external or between the frames. In Britain, because inside cylinders were favored, they were usually between the frames, and this held true even with outside cylinders. This began to change in the twentieth century, but only for a few designs. In America there was greater readiness to use outside gear. The drawback of inside gear was its poor accessibility; the complex system of rods and levers required frequent adjustment and constant lubrication, but only a contortionist could have done full justice to some of the British valve gears.

Most engineers agreed that in two-cylinder engines (the vast majority) outside cylinders were better than inside. The British were most attached to inside cylinders, arguing that they put the piston thrusts in the center, ensuring stability and reducing stresses. Others argued that outside cylinders gave better accessibility and dispensed with the expensive-to-manufacture cranked axle. Even the British favored outside cylinders for the larger locomotives in the twentieth century.

Boilers could be parallel or tapered in shape. The latter were narrower, and hence lighter, at the front, but of full girth at the firebox end, where most of the heat transfer took place. Boilers also varied in shape being domed, domeless, or multidomed. The steam dome was where steam was drawn off to be led to the cylinders. The extra height was needed in order to obtain steam with a minimum of droplets that would lower cylinder efficiency. Bury's "haystack" fireboxes of the 1840s embodied this principle, but later the dome was transferred to the boiler top. As locomotives became bigger, space for the dome was reduced, and it became flatter until some railways dispensed with it altogether. With tapered boilers, steam could be taken from the top part of the widest section of the boiler.

Sometimes the safety valve was placed at the top of the dome. Later it was most often placed above the firebox. Early safety valves used a spring-loaded lever, which was simple and easily adjusted. Later, strong springs were sufficient. The "pop" valve became popular in the twentieth century. This did not open gradually, but passed a sudden gush of steam when the pressure limit was exceeded. This had the effect of frightening passengers out of their wits, but its great advantage was that as soon as the pressure fell to the permitted limit, it cut off equally smartly. Conventional valves, once

Above: In North America the feedwater heater was usually placed ahead of the chimney, as with this Canadian National Pacific.

Left: The unusual layout of the "cab-in-front" articulated locomotives of the Southern Pacific RR. On the right is the oil-fueled firebox, and at left are the forward windows. The lower, larger gauge is the all-important steam pressure gauge. The cab-in-front was a concept specific to SP. With the chimney in the rear, exhaust was kept away from the cab, particularly useful in tunnels.

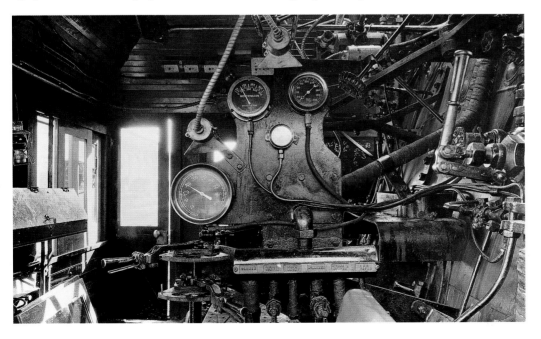

released, would close only when pressure had descended to about five pounds less than the limit, thereby wasting energy.

Many locomotives also carried a sand dome. Sanding the rails to prevent wheel-slip dates from the first years of steam traction, although initially this was simply done by a man with a bucket walking in front of the locomotive. Gravity sanding, in which sand was dropped from sandboxes and led through sandpipes to the rail-wheel interface soon followed, and toward the end of the nineteenth century the steam sander was developed. This used steam jets to impel the sand directly under the wheels. Sand was used not only when starting on wet or greasy rails but often on gradients, so a large supply was needed. From the sand dome pipes radiated down the boiler side to the individual coupled wheels, projecting sand under the wheels from both directions, so that reverse movement was also provided for. British practice was slightly different, in that the sandboxes were hidden away. Sometimes they were disguised as part of the wheel splashers, sometimes they were

Below: The 2-6-2 wheel arrangement was not common in America, but it was suited to short industrial lines where some line running as well as yard work was required. When switching, yardmen needed to ride the locomotive, and their foothold can be seen on each side of the front pilot.

attached to the frame, and the only signs of the presence of sandboxes were the lids of their filler pipes.

There were great variations in cab design, both over time and between countries. Initially, no protection was provided for the enginemen, which was one more example of the influence of coaching practice. But, if only to reduce the accident rate, a windowed screen (the spectacle plate) was soon provided in front of the footplate. The top of this was later bent back to provide an elementary roof. In North America, because of the climate and because enginemen were considered precious, the cab soon became large and enclosed, whereas in Europe, and Britain in particular, increasing comfort was a very slow process. When the North Eastern Railway, which had lines across the Pennines, equipped some of its locomotives with American-style cabs, the enginemen themselves raised a vehement protest; they saw themselves as hard men, and wanted to stay that way.

British locomotives built for export, on the other hand, carried cabs carefully designed for the conditions they would face. For hot countries with tropical storms a large-roofed, easily aired, cab was developed. In Britain itself the meager short-side and short-roof cab was gradually superseded by the side-window cab, which gave better protection. But when running backward in rain all the crews could do was unfurl a tarpaulin from roof to tender. In other countries the "tender-cab" was developed to allow for backward running; this was a cablike structure at the front of the tender.

Over the decades chimney shapes have varied, partly for aesthetic and partly for practical reasons. Very tall chimneys were a mark of the earliest engines, simply

because the taller the chimney, the better the draft. As boilers became bigger, so chimneys had to be shortened, and other ways found of maintaining sufficient draft. German locomotives had a provision for chimney extensions, so that where clearances were high an extra piece could be bolted to the basic chimney. Some locomotives of the Santa Fe Railway had an ingenious arrangement whereby the crew could raise the chimney while in motion.

The other function of the chimney was to throw exhaust clear, and especially from the line of view of the enginemen. As chimneys became smaller and trains faster, smoke and steam swirled around the cab windows, obscuring the forward view. One way around this problem was the fitting of wind-deflector plates in front of the smokebox. These did generally improve matters by creating a strong upward airflow over the front of the engine. But this was only an improvement; a perfect solution was never found. There were many styles, some tested in wind tunnels. North American railroads never adopted them on a large scale. In

fact, they were removed from several classes. In Britain, of the "Big Four" companies, the Great Western (whose chimneys tended to be somewhat taller) did not use them, but the other three companies found them worthwhile.

The outer casing of a chimney could be simple, as in the stove-pipe style, or it could be ornate, perhaps featuring a copper rim, a slim waist, and *capuchon* (a lip on the front of the cap). The quite graceful chimney that narrowed toward the middle was termed a flower-pot type (in Russia it was known as the "English Chimney"). These features made no difference to the performance of a locomotive: what was important was what was underneath the chimney. Most crucial was the arrangement by which the exhaust steam from the cylinders was led to the chimney, entraining the gases from the boiler tubes as it did so. This creation of draft was seen, as decades passed, to be both complex and important. With unimproved drafting, successive puffs of steam created a jerky draft, resulting in chunks of unburned fuel being torn from

Above: Spark arrestors diverted the exhaust downward as it left the smokebox, causing it to drop its sparks at the bottom of the arrestor before escaping to the outside. They could come in different shapes; this Austrian coal-burning locomotive on the Zillertal Railway has a chimney profile very different from old American woodburners.

Below: Serving the "Keystone State," the Pennsylvania RR used keystone-shaped front numberplates. This locomotive type is a 4-6-0 that was designed specifically for use as commuter traffic in the 1920s. Most American railroads relied on old passenger locomotives for commuter lines.

the fire and ejected into the atmosphere. During the twentieth century several devices were developed to provide a draft that was both strong and steady. These schemes divided the exhaust steam into several jets, which multiplied the surface area of the steam flows. It was this surface area that gave the pulling effect needed to create the draft.

Dividing the steam jets vertically, so that some would provide a draft for the lower tubes and others for the upper, was a comparatively early development. Dividing them horizontally came later. The most widely used device was the Kylchap exhaust, which could be recognized by the elongated chimney ("double

chimney") that accommodated the two orifices required for the two steam jets. The Lemaitre chimney had a circle of steam jets projecting upward and was characterized externally by a round, very wide chimney. Finally, at the end of the steam age and probably the best of them all (the ugliest, too) was the Giesl exhaust, in which seven jets were lined up longitudinally and fanwise, so the chimney casing was narrow and elongated. Increases of power output up to 25 percent, with some fuel savings, were claimed for the Giesl exhaust, and it was adopted in Austria, East Africa, and elsewhere. Partly because fuel economy and power-weight ratios were less important in North America, these newer drafting arrangements were little used there, although the celebrated Northern locomotives of the Union Pacific RR were an exception, some being built with, and some without, double chimneys.

The most sensible, and the most common, color for locomotives was black, but at many times and places other colors were used. In the early decades American locomotives were decorated with all kinds of intricate and colorful designs, each individual and of local creation. Sometimes, too, a name was painted on the locomotive. But later in the nineteenth century names and decoration disappeared. Latent American Puritanism was sometimes blamed for this return to plain black coloration, but the rise of accountancy seems a more likely explanation.

In Britain the individual companies, following coaching practice, used their own distinctive liveries. Various colors were used, usually of hard-wearing hues, with green the favorite. Sometimes a company would paint just its passenger locomotives in this way, leaving others plain black.

The finish of the paintwork was given high importance; a top passenger locomotive might spend two weeks in the paint shop while a dozen or more coats of paint and varnish were applied.

In the interwar years many American railroads returned to colorful liveries, at least for their best passenger locomotives. The Southern Pacific scheme was cheerful with its red and golden paneling, the Canadian Pacific displayed grey boilers, maroon paneling and golden lettering, while Canadian National locomotives looked smart in green panels with black boilers. The last U.S. main-line steam passenger trains, of the Norfolk & Western, were pulled by black locomotives sporting maroon and gold bands.

Relatively few names were carried by North American locomotives in the twentieth century, and when they appeared they were painted on, as were the locomotive numbers. In Britain named locomotives, especially in passenger service, were very common, and a given design would have its own family of names. Thus a Scottish 4-4-0 type had names taken from Walter Scott's novels painted on the splasher, while the Great Western's most celebrated class carried the names of castles, displayed on big brass nameplates. Most bizarre was the London & North

Eastern Railway, which, after bestowing the names of champion racehorses (*Pretty Polly, Galopin,* etc) on its Pacific locomotives, chose to give antelope names to a big class of post-World War II locomotives. Beginning with *Springbok* and progressing through two dozen names like *Impala, Puku,* and *Bongo,* the Company discovered that it had exhausted the antelope breeds. This gave rise to many witticisms about being impaled on the horns of a dilemma, and most of the several hundred subsequent units that were built remained nameless.

Above: Smoke deflector plates were quite rare in American practice, but the Union Pacific RR's 4-8-4 passenger locomotives carried them. They were very long, compared to European models.

Below: The Kylchap double chimney in the land of its birth. This is a French Pacific rebuilt by Chapelon.

Right: *Jupiter*, like other locomotives of that generation, burned wood in areas where a mere lineside fire could set alight a township or a forest — hence the large spark arrestor. When wood fuel was replaced by coal and oil, the need for this precaution disappeared except in a few special circumstances.

Right: A general-purpose 4-6-0 of the Mobile & Ohio Railroad. Built in 1897, only ten years after the locomotive in the lower illustration, it displays considerable advance over the latter. The spark arrestor has finally gone. The headlight, though still not electric, has been modernized, and the wheels are of a more refined design.

Below: In the 1880s many railroads were buying 2-6-0 locomotives like this for freight work. During this period there were still no locomotive brakes, reliance being placed on the tender handbrake.

Opposite, above: A postwar 2-10-2 tank locomotive design built in East Germany for the narrow gauge. The long water tanks reduce the space available for equipment, so behind the plain "stovepipe" chimney are extra domes and other equipment. The compressor for the brakes stands on one side of the smokebox.

Opposite, below: A postwar Chinese 2-8-2 locomotive. The cladding of chimney and domes, with smoke deflector plates, reflects Russian practice of the 1940s.

Below: A unique British six-wheel design built for the Southern Railway during World War II. In a spirit of wartime austerity, the boiler sheeting is the simplest possible and the wheels are without splashers. However, the design does have the luxury of a Lemaitre exhaust, with its characteristic wide chimney.

Opposite, above: The U.S. Army Transportation Corps 2-8-0 of World War II was low enough to work in Britain. This example, handed over to Polish Railways, has a chimney extension to take advantage of the more generous height limitations in that country.

Opposite, below: The Giesl exhaust, characterized by its long, flat chimney, attained greatest popularity in the land of its birth, Austria. Here an Austrian State Railways twelve-wheel tank locomotive, which was designed especially for iron-ore trains on a heavily graded route, carries one of these chimneys.

Above: The higher the chimney, the better the draft. But as boilers became bigger, chimneys became shorter. The Santa Fe Railway had an ingenious solution to this problem—a chimney-extending gear that could be operated from the cab. The chimney was raised on open stretches of line and lowered for bridges and tunnels. Only a few units of this 4-8-4 class were so fitted.

Right: A batch of newly built 2-10-2 locomotives is assembled for a publicity photograph at the Baldwin Locomotive Works. These are very characteristic U.S. locomotives, presenting a rugged image.

Below: This final 4-8-2 design for Canadian National attempted to refine the rugged image of North American locomotives. The conical front, with its recessed headlight, the shaped chimney, and the valance over the wheels all contributed to this end, as did the black, gold, and green paintwork.

Opposite: A preserved 2-10-0 operating on the Strasburg Railroad in Pennsylvania. Smokebox doors were small in America, compared to those on European locomotives. They were easier to keep airtight (very important for drafting), but they made the daily soot removal process more tedious.

Overleaf: Thirty-five of these four-cylinder compound 4-8-2 passenger locomotives were built for French Railways in 1948. Feedwater heaters are placed behind the Kylchap double chimney, and French-style inward-bent smoke deflectors are fitted. The French V-shaped cab is also shown clearly. A single safety valve is positioned immediately behind the sand dome.

Below: A 2-8-0 built by Baldwin in 1916, Engine 29 operates on the Virginia & Truckee Railroad in Nevada. Silver-painted smokebox fronts were a feature of just a few railroads, mainly in the West, although they are now quite common on tourist lines. The bracing bars running from smokebox to front beam were common on American locomotives, whose bar framing provided little resistance to frontal forces in this area.

Opposite: A Soviet Railways freight locomotive carrying the red star that was borne by all locomotives during the communist years. Several locomotives of this class carried political slogans, painted on the sides of their smoke deflectors.

Below: This Canadian Pacific locomotive carries, by permission, the British crown on its valance (it is of the "Royal Hudson" class). The chimney, though it has an elongated casing, is only an ordinary single chimney, as the exhaust indicates.

Bottom: The simplicity of a British outside-cylinder, inside-valve-gear, four-wheel tank locomotive.

Right: In the twentieth century, outside cylinders with outside valve gear became more accepted in Britain. This 2-8-0 was built by the Midland Railway workshops in 1914. The class was destined for a Midland Railway associated company, the Somerset & Dorset Joint Railway.

Opposite: Outside valve gear, inside cylinders on an Italian 2-6-0 locomotive. This arrangement was common in Italy, but rare elsewhere.

Below: Inside valve gear serving inside cylinders on a nineteenth-century British-built locomotive. This is one of the many British locomotives that the Dutch railways imported in their early decades.

Opposite, above: A Pennsylvania Railroad 2-10-4, showing the large firebox that could be supported by the rear four-wheel truck. This locomotive has Baker valve gear, which provided a wider passage for steam entering the cylinder, although this was at the cost of greater friction.

Opposite, below: Walschaerts valve gear remained the favorite on most railroads. It absorbed very little power while providing steam passages only marginally more restricted than that of the Baker gear.

Above: The Stephenson valve gear dated from the early railway age, but remained quite popular right up to the end of steam traction. Typically, it was used for British inside-cylinder designs, but in this photograph it is shown controlling the valves of a Shay vertical-cylinder locomotive.

Opposite, above: The 4-6-0, popular in the late nine-teenth-century for hauling trains that had become too heavy for the traditional 4-4-0 types, was simply an enlargement of the latter. This Baltimore & Ohio Railroad example is distinguished by a rimmed chimney and more rounded cab, but some contemporary 4-4-0s also had those features.

Opposite, below: In Britain, cabs offered little comfort. The short roof needed a supplementary weather sheet in rainy weather. This locomotive is of 1880s design; in the twentieth century bigger cabs, with side windows, appeared on the British railways.

Below: One of nearly 400 B1-class 4-6-0s of the London & North Eastern Railway, to which it was intended to affix "antelope" nameplates. In the event, only the first forty could be so honored. This is the twenty-seventh unit, Engine 1027, *Madoqua*.

THE QUEEN OF SCOTS
PULLMAN

Society on the Move

On average, railroads in North America and Europe obtained only about 10 percent of their revenue from passenger services, yet it was the latter that seemed to occupy most of the attention of both the public and the companies themselves. Heavy advertising came later in the nineteenth century, when rival companies competed along the same routes. For example, at the beginning of the twentieth century there were a half-dozen railroads offering services between New York and Chicago. Two of these lines, the New York Central and Pennsylvania, were clearly the prime operators, with their own terminals in Manhattan and their rival *Twentieth Century Limited* and *Pennsylvania Special*, but there were other companies that, for one reason or another, attracted their own clienteles. Elsewhere, there was a choice between two main routes from the Northeast to Florida, and competition was also strong between Chicago and the Pacific coast, Montreal, and Toronto, as well as between many other cities.

In Britain there were two consortia of companies operating the rival West Coast and East Coast routes between London and Scotland, and the Great Western and the London & South Western fought for the London-to-Plymouth traffic, while in Kent two other companies, the South

Eastern and the Chatham, engaged in a competitive struggle that emptied their coffers while doing little to improve services. Between Glasgow and Edinburgh, the North British and Caledonian railways fought a dour struggle. Outside Britain and the United States such competition was rare because it had been considered sensible to limit railroad construction to one line between any two cities.

Both in Britain and the United States two competing companies could emerge as the main players over a given route, but would have additional competitors with certain disadvantages, like a longer or more heavily graded route. These secondary competitors, unable to compete on speed, sought to distinguish themselves in other ways. Thus, between New York and Chicago, while the Erie RR publicized

Opposite: *Pullman trains were rare in Britain. This poster advertises the interwar Queen of Scots daytime Pullman operated by the London & North Eastern Railway between London and Scotland.*

Below: *A foot warmer in use as late as the 1970s in an unheated Australian train.*

*Above: A French
country train of the
1950s. Four-wheeled
passenger cars would
remain in service in
France and Germany
into the 1970s.*

*Below: Phoebe Snow,
the mythical passenger
of Lackawanna RR
advertising, acknow-
ledges male privileges.
The Pennsylvania State
Railroad Museum has
a collection of Phoebe
Snow posters.*

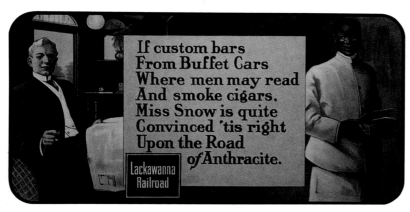

itself as an exclusive, expensively built rail-road, the Lackawanna mounted an adver-tising campaign based on a mythical character, Phoebe Snow, who traveled on the Lackawanna RR because its engines burned anthracite and therefore did not emit soot that would sully her pure-white dress. In Britain the Midland Railway was a latecomer to the Anglo-Scottish route. It could not hope to compete on speed, so provided superb rolling stock and publi-cized the scenic virtues of its route. Shortly before World War I two additional main lines were opened in Britain. A shorter Great Western line between London and Birmingham enabled the GWR to com-pete with the London & North Western, with the result that the London-to-Birmingham journey was reduced to just two hours for the 110 (GWR) and 112 (LNWR) miles. There was also the Great

Central's London extension, which brought an additional North-South com-pany to London. The GC, breaking into a market that was already satiated, could only succeed with distinctive rolling stock and heavy advertising.

During the early twentieth century the railway poster came into its own. Companies used the poster both to encourage more people to travel and to lure existing passengers from other com-panies. In Britain especially the poster campaigns gave great opportunities for promising new artists, who displayed con-siderable originality, sometimes humor, in their work. In the United States, where posters had blossomed earlier, there was more emphasis on information, and the pictorial aspect was downplayed; the typ-ical U.S. poster would be brightly col-ored and would provide information about schedules and on-board services of the trains it advertised.

To boost traffic, companies often printed guides to the localities they served. In the United States the drive by Midwestern and Western companies to attract settlers produced a flow of highly burnished handbooks and pamphlets that, more often than not, failed to distinguish between fact and fantasy. In the twenti-eth century there was greater respect for truth, and some useful holiday and tourist guides were published, to be distributed at low prices or, sometimes, free of charge.

Railroads competed with added value rather than by price-cutting. Speeding up the schedules was a prime added-value move, which sometimes resulted in a succession of speed-ups as one company sought to outpace the other. Occasionally two rival trains might move on parallel tracks, as did the New York Central and Pennsylvania trains outside Chicago, and a race could develop over a few miles. In the United States this practice was discouraged by managements, and was really nothing but a manifestation of the sporting instinct of the drivers. In Britain, the West Coast and East Coast consortia challenged each other twice in the late nineteenth century in the so-called "Railway Races." They cut the schedules of their best Anglo-Scottish trains on a daily basis, and the press reported each day on which side had made the fastest trip. Nobody asked the passengers if they enjoyed being hurled around curves in excess of speed limits or arriving at their destinations at awkward times. Sporadic racing also occurred between the London & South Western and Great Western for the transatlantic traffic bringing ocean passengers from Plymouth to London. This culminated in a derailment of a South Western train on the Salisbury curve, resulting in much loss of blood, some of it American. After this disaster, there were no more railway races.

Having some overlap in religious traditions, both the United States and Britain were scenes of conflict between the railroad companies and those who felt that all trains should remain motionless on Sundays. In the United States local Sabbath committees were active through-out most of the second half of the nineteenth century, accusing managements of godlessness, and regarding Sunday travel by women as the ultimate degradation. For the most part the railroads made compromises without, however, entirely stopping Sunday operations. Sometimes passengers were required to give a pledge that their travel was vitally necessary, and there were odd occasions upon which, having failed to reach its destination by Saturday midnight, a train was required to remain stationary for 24 hours. In Britain the Sabbatarian movement persuaded most companies to reduce the scale of their operations on Sundays, but never succeeded in closing the system down. Eventually, a kind of tacit understanding evolved: by 1914 about one-fifth of the railway mileage was closed to passengers on Sundays; elsewhere passenger trains ran, but only rarely and slowly. So in Britain there were separate timetables for Sunday services (which remains the case today). What became known as the Railway Sunday certainly discouraged people from traveling on their day of leisure, but this, most likely, increased alcohol consumption more than religious devotion.

Below: In difficult times, when passengers are too many and trains too few, some passengers have to travel outside the train. At other times, it is one way of evading ticket purchase. This 1970s picture is from India.

Above: *A small station west of Laramie, Wyoming. The locomotive sports a set of antlers. Deer and other animals could come to grief either through collisions or the hunting activities of train crews.*

As with so much else, the coaching traditions were carried forward into the early design of passenger vehicles, which tended to resemble road coaches mounted on a railway frame and wheels. Gradually a more specific railroad style developed, but there was an early divergence between American and European practice. While European railways, including the British, stayed with rigid-wheelbase vehicles of four and six wheels, the Americans soon standardized the eight-wheel car riding on two pivoted trucks. The Baltimore & Ohio had such vehicles as early as 1831. They gave a smoother ride, especially over low-grade track, and it is not surprising that the first British railway to adopt this style, in 1870, was a narrow-gauge line — the Ffestiniog Railway. In America the center-aisle open car was used, whereas in Europe the compartment car was favored.

In the late nineteenth century the British and other European railways turned toward the eight-wheeler, but held onto their preference for compartments. Side corridors were slowly introduced from the 1890s, making the provision of washrooms practicable for all passengers and, in a growing number of trains, giving access to a dining car. Connections between

cars were an American development. Originally, the American eight-wheelers were boarded at open platforms, or verandas, at each end of the car, and it was not long before these platforms were fully enclosed to form vestibules, with a concertina connection between adjacent cars.

The price of an American long-distance rail journey was the sum of the transportation rate (the basic fare, which included a seat in "coach class") and various accommodation supplements. Accommodation could vary from a grand bedroom through the ordinary berth cars to a seat in the observation, or parlor, car. These accommodations were the equivalent of the European First Class, open only to those who had paid the extra money. Parlor cars provided exclusive accommodation on day trains. They were generally marshaled at the rear of the train, providing a good rearward view. Armchairs, and sometimes writing tables and a bar, were provided.

In Britain, as early as 1874, the Midland Railway in its quest for a competitive edge imported some Pullman twelve-wheel day coaches, followed by sleepers. But in general the British stayed with their own conventions, although a domestic Pullman company was founded that operated Pullman chair cars on a few selected services.

Parliament had compelled the British companies in 1844 to provide a daily cheap train with roofed rolling stock over all their lines, so as to make it possible for the not-so-rich to use the railway (the imposed penny-per-mile fare was still not cheap enough for the poor). These "parliamentary trains" were notoriously slow at first, but gradually Third Class service was developed, which more than met the "parliamentary" requirement. First Class was opulent, and Second Class was for those who did not want to lower themselves to Third Class but were not elevated enough to travel by First. Some railways in India and Russia provided a Fourth Class for the very poor. Prussia provided a Military Class.

In the United States those who possessed nothing but a sense of adventure traveled free by jumping onto trains. The best place was between the rear of the locomotive tender and the first car, which on passenger trains was a baggage car without an end window through which the illicit traveler might be observed. Thousands of hobos (those wandering in search of work) and tramps (those just wandering) climbed aboard American trains every day. Train crews were instructed to get rid of them, which they did, sometimes with unnecessary violence. At other times a blind eye might be turned. The railroads regarded these unwanted travelers as a great expense, not because of the lost revenue they represented but because they caused so much damage to freight consignments.

A number of Americans designed sleeping cars, but it was George Pullman who eventually dominated this field, his pull-down upper berth being the foundation of his success. Until the U.S. Government obliged the Pullman Company, on anti-monopoly grounds, to divest itself of its operating function, Pullman not only built sleeping and dining cars but also operated them with its own staff. For a long period, the job of Pullman porter (car attendant) was about the only position with prospects open to African Americans. In Canada, as late as the mid-twentieth century, the irreverent conventional wisdom held that any black student seen on a university campus must be either a foreigner or the son of a Pullman porter.

In Britain sleeping cars, which initially tended to carry just a dozen First Class passengers, were a high-cost service, and the supplementary fare did not cover this. As a small country, Britain did not really need sleeping cars; they were simply an extra, optional service to be found mainly on the London-to-Scotland routes, to Holyhead in northwest Wales (for the Irish

Left: The Santa Fe RR, like many other railroads, built its own hotels. This one, the luxury "El Tovar," was also part of the company's endeavors to develop the Grand Canyon as a vacation destination for its passengers.

ferry traffic) and to Devon and Cornwall. An innovation in the 1920s was the provision of sleeping cars for Third Class passengers; they paid a supplement and were provided with just a pillow and blanket.

Sleeping cars had relatively little application in continental Europe, although the Wagons-Lit Company operated them in several famous international trains, like the *Orient Express*, that were definitely in the deluxe category. Outside Russia, internal sleeper services were few, Paris-to-Marseilles being perhaps the best example. French railways exploited the *couchette*, in which seats were converted to berths. With six berths per compartment and a supplementary fare added to the normal tariff, these cars could make a profit.

In Britain the Midland Railway, ever seeking innovations to increase its share of the market, caused a great disturbance in 1872 when it announced that all its trains, including the fastest, would offer Third Class accommodation. It followed this by renaming Second Class as Third Class and abolishing the old Third Class. This made Third a very attractive bargain for the majority of travelers. The

other companies grumbled but slowly had to follow the MR's example. The chairman of the Lancashire & Yorkshire Railway, in other respects an innovative company, condemned the change as "Americanization" that would result in well-dressed people traveling Third Class. Eventually the only Second Class accommodation was to be found on boat trains to the Channel ports, to provide for continental Europeans traveling on Second Class tickets issued by their own railroads. Finally, in 1956, Third Class was renamed Second Class in Britain, and corresponded to the Coach Class of North America and Economy Class of some other railroads.

Ladies-only compartments were provided by some British companies and could be also found elsewhere. In Pakistan, until quite recent times, regulations allowed a lady traveling alone in First Class to take along for protection a servant or dog (but not both). In the early railroad decades, especially in compartmented stock, women were at the mercy of obnoxious fellow-travelers. But there were technical problems in providing an alarm system in each

Below: The United States railroads developed a superb baggage-checking system that was later copied by the airlines. This is the baggage-handling hall at Los Angeles Union Terminal.

compartment. Belgian railways had staff patrolling the outside of trains, clambering along the footboards while the train was in motion; the number of fatalities and injuries suffered by these men probably outnumbered the murders and indecent assaults they discouraged.

When it was thought that a reliable alarm system had been discovered, Britain's Board of Trade obliged companies to provide an alarm in each compartment. Despite a heavy fine payable by passengers "for improper use," the companies remained reluctant, and when the favored system proved to be a failure they adopted all kinds of cheap and generally useless devices in order to satisfy, on paper, the unwanted regulation. But eventually the "alarm chain" was generally adopted. This was connected to the guard's handbrake so, in an emergency, a passenger could make a brake application. The same system was adopted by several other countries. In North America the open center-aisle vehicle, plus the provision of single-sex rest areas—where men could (among other things) spit and women could (among other things) breastfeed—avoided many of the problems encountered in other countries.

Since, prior to steam train travel, stage coaches had not been heated, there was no immediate call for train heating. Footwarmers came into use, with the typical British company supplying them free to First Class passengers and later allowing other classes to hire them (although the Lancashire & Yorkshire Railway long resisted the supply of foot warmers to the lower classes). As in so many aspects of passenger accommodation, America led the way, providing woodburning stoves at an early stage. Steam heating, in which steam from the locomotive was piped

down the trains, was also an American innovation of the 1880s; it became standard practice in Europe, and in the twentieth century all British steam trains had steam heat. Britain introduced electric train lighting in 1881, slightly in advance of the United States.

Compulsory fitting of passenger trains with automatic brakes also occurred in America before the British railways were compelled to do the same. The resistance of the British companies to this life-saving but expensive innovation was notorious, and delighted Marxist agitators. On the other hand, despite the high cost (not only of fitting but also of sacrificing seating space) the British companies were not unduly slow in providing toilets. The extension of nonstop services was seen as making such provision unavoidable.

Mail, parcels, and baggage are also categorized as passenger traffic. In North America these were carried at the head end of a train, often in a "combination" car providing separate accommodation for each category and also a place for the baggage handler. Mail was carried by

Above: By most definitions the first locomotive to be built with streamlining was this Milwaukee RR Atlantic of 1934. With three similar units, it hauled the Hiawatha trains between Chicago and Minneapolis/St. Paul, and frequently exceeded 100 mph.

Above: *The London to Paris Golden Arrow was a service consisting of two trains linked by a ferry. This is the locomotive of the French train, with its* Fleche d'Or *headboard.*

contract with the Post Office; the rate was low but it was an assured daily income. In the 1950s the end of a mail contract was often the final financial blow that sealed the fate of a passenger train or secondary line. Sorting the mail on the train by Post Office employees became popular on some routes both in Britain and the United States. In Britain the first such "traveling post office" operated between Liverpool and Birmingham in 1838, and in America on the Terre Haute & Richmond RR in 1855. In Britain the Chester & Holyhead Railway was built specifically to handle mail, and became the route of the *Irish Mail*. In the United States the "Fast Mail" between New York and Chicago was the first all-mail train. Such trains exchanged mail pouches at places en route without stopping, the pouches being suspended on arms and caught in nets. Many mail trains had passenger accommodation attached, and were the fastest trains on the line.

Parcel traffic on the early American railways was handled by entrepreneurs who acted as couriers, making regular trips and charging for the packages they took as baggage. Later they formed bigger organizations, called express companies; American Express started in that way. Eventually, by means of purchases and mergers, the Railway Express Agency evolved, jointly owned by the American railroads.

In Britain the train's guard was in charge of parcels and any mail pouches, together with passengers' bicycles and baby carriages. There was at least one guard's van at the tail end of the train, usually forming part of a passenger coach. This had the guard's hand-brake, desk, and space for mail, parcels, and baggage. To the British passenger, the guard was simply the official who waved his green flag to start the train and then jumped on while it was moving out. In fact, he had a number of other important functions and, like the American conductor, was the person in charge of the train.

During the nineteenth century certain trains that had run regularly for years and offered a superior service acquired names, at first unofficially and then deliberately as part of an advertising strategy. In Britain the East Coast *Flying Scotsman* was one of these; in the 1870s it was averaging 48 miles per hour for the first 75 miles of its London-to-Edinburgh run. In the United States, passenger trains were generally lethargic until the 1880s, but during the next twenty years there was a transformation. The best New York-to-Chicago service, which had averaged little more than 30 miles per hour in the 1870s and provided a 25-hour trip in the 1880s, had by 1905 been reduced to 18 hours. The reduced duration was achieved by the rival New York Central and Pennsylvania *Twentieth Century Limited* and *Pennsylvania Special* (which later became the *Broadway Limited*). In practice, 18 hours was somewhat strenuous, and the two companies later agreed to ease the deadline. But in 1938 the *Twentieth Century Limited*, steam-hauled until 1945, was on a 16-hour schedule. In Canada the Canadian National and Canadian Pacific decided during the Interwar period that their fierce schedule-cutting on the Montreal-to-Toronto run was excessive and agreed to operate the route jointly with "pool trains." This, sensible in the circumstances, would have been impossible in the United States with its antimonopoly legislation.

Speed was not a main factor in the competitive battle between the transcontinental companies. With such long transits, comfort was what counted, and each company tried to outdo the others in this respect. Yet North American railroads did not offer a true transcontinental service, with the exception at some periods of a secondary link between Miami and Los Angeles. The celebrated trains to the Pacific started at Chicago, where passengers from the East had to change trains and, usually, depots. But, while

there were no coast-to-coast passenger cars, there were coast-to-coast freight cars, a situation giving rise to the celebrated remark that it was easier for a pig than a human to cross the United States by train. Similarly, in Canada the transcontinentals started not on the Atlantic Coast, but at Montreal and Toronto. In Russia, however, after the Trans Siberian railroad was completed in the early twentieth century, it was possible to travel from the Baltic Sea to the Pacific without changing trains. (Australians were less fortunate; their transcontinental link was plagued by change-of-gauge problems).

On rare occasions a special train would run all the way across the United States. The president of the Union Pacific RR once rode from San Francisco (Oakland) to New York, covering the 3,344 miles in 71 hours, 27 minutes, which seems to have remained the steam-age record.

The most widely celebrated American competition in the early 1900s was that between the Pennsylvania and Reading Railroads over the Camden

Below: In the later nineteenth century the twelve-wheel passenger car became popular in the United States for its steady riding qualities. This is a Union Pacific example, built in that railroad's own shops in Omaha, Nebraska.

(near Philadelphia) -to-Atlantic City route. This was only a short trip (55 miles for one company, 58 miles for the other), and after the Pennsylvania had relaid its line for high-speed running, competitive schedule cutting resulted in 60 miles per hour average speeds; that meant the trains ran at 70 miles per hour for much of the distance. British commentators were equally struck by the *Empire State Express* of the New York Central, which covered the 440 miles from New York to Buffalo in 8-1/4 hours, whereas the equivalent run in Britain (London-to-Perth, Scotland, also 440 miles) could only be done in 9 hours.

In the early twentieth century a number of speed records were claimed by U.S. railroads, but these were never officially confirmed. The celebrated No 999 of the New York Central, for example, achieved a very high speed hauling the *Empire State Express*, but whether it was really 112 miles per hour has been doubted. The first properly authenticated 100 miles per hour of a U.S. steam locomotive was that of the Milwaukee RR's No 6402 in 1934, which touched 103.5 miles per hour. Similarly, in Britain the Great Western's *City of Truro* was timed

Below: In 1899 the feuding South Eastern and London Chatham & Dover railways joined to form the South Eastern & Chatham. This is one of the newly formed organization's advertising postcards.

at 102 miles per hour during the Ocean Mails "race," but subsequent research cast doubts on the precise speed attained.

Between the Wars, train speeds increased markedly and were intensively publicized. In the early 1930s the British *Cheltenham Flyer*, whose *Castle*-class locomotive once averaged 81 miles per hour start-to-stop over 77 miles, claimed the title of "world's fastest train," only to be challenged by a Canadian Pacific Montreal-to-Toronto service. Then came a British streamliner, the *Coronation*, but the American streamliners were winning the honors in the late 1930s. The streamlined steam *Hiawatha* of the Milwaukee RR normally exceeded 100 miles per hour over parts of its daily run between Chicago and St Paul. In Britain both the East Coast and West Coast routes had their streamliners, and the 393-mile London-to-Edinburgh schedule was brought down to 6 hours in 1937 with the London & North Eastern Railway's *Coronation*. It was an East Coast streamlined locomotive, *Mallard*, that at the cost of a melted bearing won the final steam speed record of 125 miles per hour while undergoing brake trials in 1938. A German streamliner had briefly held the record, 124.5 miles per hour achieved on a test run in 1935.

Luxury trains, as opposed to high-speed trains, also attracted a following. In North America they were to be found on the several American and Canadian transcontinental routes. South Africa had its *Blue Train*, between Johannesburg and Capetown, that was usually fully booked weeks in advance. In Australia the Sydney-to-Melbourne route was handicapped by a break of gauge, but during the 1930s the Victorian Railways took passengers in great comfort aboard the

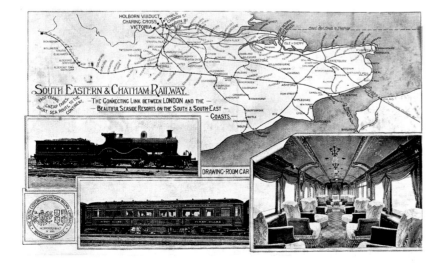

Spirit of Progress from Melbourne as far as Albury. There was also an Australian transcontinental train operated by Commonwealth Railways at an average speed of 28 miles per hour, and carrying a grand piano in its parlor car. The Trans Siberian train of Soviet Railroads was even slower, and had lost the piano it carried in tsarist days.

Providing opportunity to many to live where the air was fresh or enjoy an annual holiday away from home, the railways brought great benefits. Much of the social effect of railroad passenger travel was not so much a revolution but an extension of opportunities. Long-distance travel existed before the railroads in the form of the ocean-going ship. Holiday resorts were beginning to develop before the railways. A few people were already beginning to live at a distance from their place of work. But these tendencies accelerated greatly with the rise of the railways, and were exploited not just by the rich. The development of outer suburbs, or "dormitory towns," would hardly have been possible without the railways. Many holiday resorts, like America's Atlantic City and Miami, England's Weston-super-Mare and Blackpool, and Nice, France, would not have developed without the presence of the railroad and, in many cases, the railroads' efforts to boost them. Railway-owned hotels soon appeared, in many cases setting new standards of comfort and hygiene. At first they were built in cities, usually at the railway station. Later the railway resort hotel appeared. These, with some exceptions, were not at the seaside but at quiet spots served by the railroad. Thus was born the concept of the country-house hotel. In Scotland the railways built hotels linked with golf courses, as at Gleneagles.

In the United States the Santa Fe Railway invested heavily in the Grand Canyon, while the Union Pacific did much for the development of the Yellowstone resorts.

The last intercity steam trains ran in Britain between London and Bournemouth in 1968. In the United States the Norfolk & Western was operating its steam semistreamlined *Powhatan Arrow* and *Pocahontas* between Cincinnati, Ohio, and Norfolk, Virginia, in the late 1950s, and steam commuter services survived on the Grand Trunk Western at Detroit until 1960. The Canadian Pacific maintained steam commuter trains out of Montreal into the early 1960s. In Australia there was a daily steam-hauled outer suburban run into Newcastle until 1971. The last steam passenger trains in India were disappearing in the late 1990s. In China, at the dawn of the twenty-first century, it was still possible to travel long-distance behind a steam locomotive.

Above: *A Canadian Pacific transcontinental train enters Banff Station in the Rockies, hauled by one of the massive "Selkirk" 2-10-4 locomotives designed especially for this mountainous section of the line.*

Above: The *Scarborough Flyer*, an English seaside resort train of the London & North Eastern Railway.

Right: What the British railways called "through carriages" are attached to an Inverness-bound train at a lonely junction. Their journey originated in Thurso, at the northern extremity of Scotland.

Overleaf, page 110, above: A Belgian commuter train. The long foot boards could be used by traveling ticket inspectors to move down the train.

Overleaf, below: The streamlined *20th Century Limited* of the New York Central skirts the Hudson River.

Page 111, above: America's last steam streamliner. The Norfolk & Western Railroad's *Powhatan Arrow* prepares to leave Cincinnati for Norfolk, Virginia, in 1957.

Above: The still-incomplete Union Pacific Railroad offers its passenger service, with Wells Fargo coach connections providing onward service from its temporary terminus at North Platte.

Right: Populating the West. The B & M RR was one of several offering discount tickets for passengers scouting for landholdings. Both pictures on this page illustrate how much information could be crammed into American railroad posters.

Opposite: A publication celebrating an unprecedented fast run on the Santa Fe RR. In 1905 the businessman Walter Scott hired a three-car special train that covered the 2,265 miles from Los Angeles to Chicago in just under 45 hours.

Above: El Navajo Hotel at Gallup in New Mexico, built jointly by the Santa Fe RR and the Harvey restaurant and hotel company. The two companies were closely associated in their efforts to boost tourism in the Southwest, and they set high standards. Mary E.J. Colter, the Harvey Company's resident architect, incorporated native Navajo themes in the design and interior fittings of this building. This landmark, considered by many to be Colter's finest building, was demolished in the 1930s.

Opposite: One of the most magnificent railroad resort hotels, the Canadian Pacific's Banff Springs Hotel in the Alberta Rockies. The railroad lines were effective in promoting the scenic attractions of then-remote areas of the North American West, which they made viable as tourist destinations. For some years such hotels did boost railroad passenger traffic, but eventually most of their guests came by other forms of transportation.

Opposite, above left: A Danish poster, designed to attract English-speaking passengers to a new fast train, and foreshadowing the diesel era.

Opposite, above right: The standard Russian passenger locomotive figures in this poster showing the railway targets for the first Soviet Five-Year Plan.

Opposite, below: Just like ocean liners, the smartest international trains had their own luggage labels.

Above: The London Midland & Scottish Railway commissioned the well-known commercial artist Norman Wilkinson to produce this poster showing its new Anglo-Scottish streamliner climbing Shap Fell, in northern England.

Below: Blackpool was Britain's best-known seaside resort, and even the Great Central Railway, which did not have a station there, advertised its attractions.

DRAWING ROOM CAR-FOLKESTONE EXPRESS
SOUTH EASTERN & CHATHAM RAILWAY

Previous pages, page 118: A parlor car, or club car, built in the mid-1930s by American Car & Foundry.

Page 119: A traditional Pullman diner built in 1930 and soon to be superseded by more modern designs.

Opposite, above: An interior view of an old restored Pullman parlor car.

Opposite, below: The Pullman parlor-car concept in southeastern England, as used in the 70-mile London-to-Folkestone service.

Right: A British Third-Class six-wheeler of the late nineteenth century. This example belonged to the Midland Railway.

Below: With wide windows, and coupled to the rear of a train, the parlor car became the observation car. This example was used in the Southern Pacific's San Francisco-to-Portland "Daylight" service.

Above: An early Harvey House at Syracuse in Kansas. The Harvey station restaurants, aimed at western rail travelers, soon established a reputation for meticulousness, reliability, and culinary innovation. The "Harvey Girls" enjoyed the same kind of status as air hostesses half a century later.

Opposite: Pullman car passengers are checked in at their departure station. This Southern Pacific publicity picture was made in about 1935; the posters show both steam and diesel traction.

Opposite, above: The Pennsylvania Railroad had its tunnel into Manhattan, but other lines arriving on the New Jersey shore ferried their passengers across, with freight cars floated over, hauled by tugs. By the end of the steam age the railroad passenger ferries across the Hudson had practically disappeared, although freight cars continued to be handled at ferry wharves like this.

Opposite, below: In Britain, the best passenger trains carried long wooden destination boards. These slotted into place and could be changed easily. Each company had its own style of lettering and color.

Above: Mail exchange gear on a Traveling Post Office operated in a British mail train. The net catches a mail pouch suspended at the lineside.

Left: A First-Class vehicle dating from the early years of France's Nord Railway. The influence of stage coach practice on early railway car design is evident.

Freight

Some early railway lines were designed for passenger traffic but soon found an additional role as freight carrier. Many more were designed for freight traffic from the start. These included the single-purpose lines built to gain access to a particular natural resource. The many lines from the coast into the interiors of Africa, South America, Australia, and elsewhere were among these. They are examples of the railroad in its prime function of low-cost bulk carrier. Rail costs were much lower than highway costs, and although ship and barge costs were even lower, water transportation was slow, could freeze up in winter, and was simply not available in most locations. However, there were notable exceptions that did present effective competition for the railroads, like the St. Lawrence Seaway and Great Lakes and the Mississippi River in North America, and the Danube and Volga Rivers in Europe.

In the United States the Norfolk & Western and its neighbor the Virginian RR were almost single-commodity lines, hauling coal across the mountains and down to tidewater. The eighteenth-century horse railways of northeastern England had had a similar function, although they were shorter and their trains were only a fraction of the weight of the U.S. trains.

In addition to the big American coal-haulers, coal was the lifeblood of many railroads elsewhere. Small companies in South Wales brought loaded trains down from the mining valleys to the port city of Cardiff. In India the East Indian Railway, having fostered the development of coal-fields near Calcutta, was then bitterly criticized both for its high tariffs and its take-it-or-leave-it attitude. Coal traffic amounted to 28 percent of the total in Russia in the mid-1950s, while in Britain it was more than half.

With regular bulk freight providing a secure revenue, railroads could develop other business. Apart from passengers, there were the so-called high-value freights, or merchandise. This was not bulk traffic and needed individual handling, often as carload or less-than-car-

Opposite: *The railroad as bulk carrier: oil tank trains being assembled in a Southern Pacific yard at Beaumont, Texas. Most of this traffic is now handled by pipeline, although some refined products are still sent by train.*

Below: *A country freight station in New South Wales, Australia. The daily exchange of freight cars is in progress.*

Above: The first freight locomotive used by the Denver & Rio Grande RR, put into service in 1871. The smaller wheels and extra driving axle made it more suitable for pulling heavy loads than the general-purpose 4-4-0 type.

load shipments. But the extra cost of handling was more than compensated by the high tariffs that could be levied; ideally, a railroad sought to charge "what the traffic will bear," that is, to keep the tariff high, but not so high as to limit the market for the product.

Sometimes rightly, sometimes wrongly, the railways were accused of abusing their monopoly situation. In the United States such resentment gave birth to the Granger Movement of farmers opposed not only to railroad tariff policies but also to the arrogant attitude of railroad bosses. Having gained political influence, the movement persuaded the government to

intervene. Government regulation of rates and conditions was a feature of most other countries. This supervision was probably beneficial at the time, but when the railroads lost their monopoly with the increased capacity and economy of highway traffic, government regulations deprived them of the tariff flexibility they needed to combat the new competition.

In the United States the Interstate Commerce Commission was clearly hampering efficient railroad operation during the last decades of steam. For example, it deterred one railroad from introducing larger grain cars by declaring that the resultant reduced costs (and tariffs) would constitute "unfair competition" for the parallel river transportation companies. In Canada the "Crow's Nest" grain rates imposed by the government were helpful to agriculture, but meant that the enormous effort made by the railroads to handle the three-month grain peak went unrewarded (making sure that there were enough empty grain cars was one big problem). In Britain the interwar railways were similarly hampered by Board of Trade regulations which, however wise they may have been in the nineteenth century, could only frustrate the railways in their struggle against highway operators. The latter, in Britain, the United States, and elsewhere, naturally "skimmed the cream," aiming at the railroads' high-value, high-revenue merchandise traffic.

At the beginning of the twentieth century the U.S. railroads seemed to have developed the most efficient ways of handling freight traffic, and these lasted into the post-Steam Era. With the exception of the Long Island RR, U.S. companies made more money from freight than from passenger operations. Indeed, some companies made a loss on their passenger side, although their accounting procedures were not always capable of revealing this. The basis of U.S. operations was the railroad division, typically about 100 miles long. The "division points" (at division junctions) usually had locomotive depots, inspection tracks, and sorting ("classification") yards. The employees' schedules gave times for trains over the division, although only the schedules of First Class trains (including the few types of freight allowed to run at passenger train speeds) would be adhered to rigidly. The next category of freight was the "symbol" or "manifest" train—regular trains operating on moderately fast schedules and intended for merchandise and other time-sensitive loads. But much of the traffic was handled by "extras." Despite their name, some of these ran every day, but there was no obligation to do so. They carried most of the bulk loads, ran rather slowly, were often known as "drags," and were given lowest priority when things went wrong.

At the big classification yards near junctions, incoming trains would be broken up, and their vehicles directed to tracks where new trains to particular onward destinations would be assembled.

Classification cost time and money, so there was a clear advantage to running complete trains from origin to destination without intermediate sorting, and great administrative efforts were made to increase the number of such trains. Coal from mine to seaport or generating plant, ore from quarry to blast furnace, were obvious candidates for this treatment. Conversely, the single shipment occupying perhaps only a part of a freight car's capacity was a high-cost operation, very vulnerable to highway competition.

The local pick-up freight train ("wayfreight" in North America, "local goods" in Britain) had an important role, picking up and depositing freight cars at any station that had at least a reception track. Such a track was sufficient, say, for consignments of house-coal or fertilizer, which could be unloaded by the consignee direct from freight car to highway vehicle or trackside dump. But larger settlements would have a fully fledged freight depot, including a covered loading platform and storage space, and usually a crane. Railways offered their own pickup and delivery service to clients, maintaining their own carts and, later, motor

Opposite, below:
Freight trains pass on the through roads at Patna station, East India, in the 1970s. The British left India with a highly developed railway system, which became a key element in the post-independence drive to industrialization.

Left: A Canadian Pacific local freight climbs out of St John, New Brunswick. The 2-8-0 locomotive is running tender-first, which on most railroads was acceptable only for short distances and at moderate speeds.

Above: *A British freight train with its guard's van, or brake van. The photograph dates from the 1960s, a transition time for British Railways, with steam giving way to diesel and, as on one platform here, "bus-stop" shelters replacing traditional structures at wayside stations.*

delivery trucks. Typically, a local freight depot would be visited once daily by the local freight train, whose locomotive would perform the required yard work, placing the vehicles it was dropping off and picking up newly loaded cars before setting off for the next station on the line. Those cars would be deposited eventually in a classification yard for dispatch as part of a long-distance train. Toward the end of the Steam Era, these local services were diminishing, being high-cost, low-revenue, operations; the smaller depots were closed, with those that survived serving a larger area by means of increased use of highway trucks.

By 1900 the U.S. railroads were well on the way toward complete adoption of the Westinghouse automatic brake, which enabled trains to move faster, and the automatic coupling which, apart from speeding yard operations and saving lives, was a much stronger assembly, thereby enabling heavier trains to be operated without the fear of coupler breakage. In Britain these two processes were finished only some years after the retirement of the last steam locomotive. In continental Europe and most of the British Empire screw couplings were in general use; they had a fair safety record, though they were

time-consuming, and they were considered adequate. However, Soviet Railways, with its need to operate very heavy bulk freight trains, opted to follow the American example.

The British freight car, unlike the American flexible-truck eight-wheeler, ran on a two-axle rigid wheelbase and carried a small load of 10 to 20 tons. Freight cars were loose-coupled by chains slung over a drawhook. When a British freight train started to move, there would be a succession of metallic rumbles as each coupler took up the slack. Most freight cars had lever brakes, applied by a railwayman standing at the trackside. These brakes could be pinned down at the crest of a steep descent, but otherwise were scarcely used. At the tail end of the train was the guard's van, often ballasted, and this had a hand brake that could be operated by the guard in accordance with set routines or when the train's driver signaled with blasts from the locomotive whistle. Avoiding massive jerks over sawtooth grades was a skilled technique, requiring good understanding between driver and guard, each controlling his own brake.

Loose coupling was archaic and costly, in terms of time, money, and physical injury. But a conversion to automatic couplings would have required more investment than British companies were willing to undertake, and in the changeover period, rolling stock would need to be fitted with both types of coupling. Uniquely, in 1925 the Japanese State Railways surprised the world by a virtual overnight conversion to automatic couplings. The secret behind this was an eight-year preparation period and, in the weeks preceding the change, the loading of the new couplings into every freight car. On the big day, which was a holiday with reduced freight traffic, gangs descended on each freight car and changed the couplings.

The United States had a much lower proportion of independently owned freight cars than Britain. The latter was exceptional, with more than 40 percent of the freight car stock, about 600,000 units, belonging to more than 4,000 different owners in 1939. These vehicles, belonging mostly to colliery companies, had their own liveries and were not maintained by the railway companies. They were often inefficiently small, badly lubricated, and susceptible to breakdown. Moreover, their owners were unwilling to replace them with bigger, more efficient, units. The independently owned coal vehicles were requisitioned during World War II, giving improved utilization (they could carry a return load, instead of being returned empty direct to the colliery), but it was only the nationalization of the British coal companies that finally solved the problem.

Meanwhile, other independently owned vehicles, like the banana vans owned by Fyffes and the chocolate vans owned by various manufacturers, were resplendent in their eye-catching liveries. In North America the most noticeable such cars were those used by fruit companies, which were brightly painted in yellows and oranges. Fruit trains were operated from California and Florida to the big cities of the Eastern Seaboard and Midwest. A feature of this fruit traffic was that loaded cars could, at the request of the shipper, be redirected en route to destinations where fruit prices were rising. Other significant users of their own (or sometimes leased) vehicles were the Midwestern meat processors. Like the fruit industry, the meat industry benefited from the introduction of the ice-packed refrigera-

tor car. Instead of being shipped from the Great Plains in expensive-to-run cattle trains, animals were slaughtered in prime condition where they were raised, and then frozen for shipment to the Chicago, Illinois, meat-packers.

Perishables eventually became a major traffic for some railways. Growers in Cornwall, western England, were able to market flowers and early vegetables in London. Special glass-lined tank cars were introduced so that the product of the evening milking in Devon and Wiltshire (in southwestern England) could be delivered to Londoners' doorsteps the next morning. Fish, packed with ice in boxes, was also an important cargo for some British railways. There were regular fish

Above: A British private-owner coal wagon. In service, the paintwork of such cars was soon submerged beneath a layer of black grime.

Below: At Paddington Station, one of London's largest terminals, a fish van is removed from the tail-end of an arriving passenger train, for unloading at a nearby fish platform.

Above: Before special "auto-rack" cars were introduced, new automobiles were shipped in box-cars. Despite the wide doors, loading and unloading was a time-consuming, labor-intensive process.

trains from northern ports to London, leaving a trail of fishy smells and melted ice as they passed. Smaller fish shipments, loaded into a four-wheeler, were often attached to the ends of passenger trains. In Argentina, the Buenos Aires Great Southern operated overnight fruit trains from the Rio Negro Valley to Buenos Aires. These trains weighed about 1,000 tons and ran at passenger-train speeds. In South Africa, "apple specials" were operated by narrow-gauge lines for the benefit of the export trade.

Locomotives specifically designed for fast freights appeared in the United States, especially during the 1920s when highway competition for merchandise traffic was becoming evident. To compete with the truckers, the railroads ran regular scheduled fast freights, or "hotshots." To maintain high speeds over long distances, a reliable high-horsepower output was needed. This implied a big firegrate, and several designs appeared, recognizable by the four-wheel truck supporting the enlarged grate. The 2-8-4 wheel arrangement became quite popular for these trains, although most companies invested in 4-8-4 types that they used both for passenger and fast freight work.

In other countries the same locomotive need was satisfied by the growing popularity of the "mixed-traffic" engine, suitable for most passenger trains and for freight. In Britain, this was usually a 2-6-0 or 4-6-0, while in France and Germany the 2-8-2 arrangement became the standard for these trains, the more traditional 2-8-0 and 2-10-0 wheel arrangements being retained for heavier, slower trains. But in continental Europe the fast freight never became as common as in Britain and North America, partly because there were multinational controls restricting highway operators. In Soviet Russia good-quality highways and fast freights were equally unknown.

In Britain the need for fast freights brought with it the need for automatically braked freight cars; otherwise high speeds could be dangerous. Some freight cars were fitted with screw couplings and the vacuum automatic brake, as used on passenger vehicles, and a number of these "fitted" vehicles would be marshaled next to the engine. Fast freights were classified into those with up to one-third, and those with more than one-third, of fitted cars. Another way around the braking problem was the parcels train, which was classed as a passenger train and used passenger-style rolling stock, eight-wheeled and vacuum-braked. It carried parcels, some less-than-carload shipments, and might also include milk tank cars and mail vehicles.

Notable examples of fast high-value freight trains were the "silkers" that carried Japanese raw silk to the U.S. silk industry. This was an exceptionally high-value freight, so an additional advantage of high speed was the reduced period of insurance coverage that was needed. Canadian and U.S. railroads competed for this traffic, which crossed the Pacific from Yokohama and was destined for New York. The Canadian National broke into the market in 1925, its first silk train from Vancouver consisting of eight paper-lined baggage cars that carried not only the bales but also armed guards. By the end of the decade the CN was running ten-car silk trains at speeds faster than the passenger service.

In Britain the silk traffic followed a different pattern, with stocks held in London sent in frequent small shipments to purchasers, usually by overnight fast freight. The fast freight had been a feature of the British railways since at least the 1850s. Because distances were short, the railways could offer overnight delivery almost anywhere, the ideal being that a businessman from the provinces could visit one or other London commodity market and return home the same day, with his purchase shipped by night train so as to be available to him the next morning. Over the trunk routes out of London a succession of fast freights left in the hours preceding midnight, and a succession of arrivals followed in the early hours of the morning. By 1914 some British companies were operating fully braked trains at an average of 40 miles per hour. Between the wars these services were extended and improved, largely because of highway competition but also because of the rise of new small-scale industries with their frequent time-sensitive shipments.

The fast overnight freight, carrying whatever merchandise traffic could be attracted, became a feature of U.S. railroads in the 1930s, the first example being, probably, the Cotton Belt RR *Blue Streak* of 1931. Chicago and the big cities on the Eastern Seaboard were main beneficiaries of these new trains, some of which had special paint schemes.

The average U.S. long-distance freight was also accelerated in the interwar years. Average train weight grew, so the key statistic "net ton-miles per train-hour" improved from 10,580 in 1929 to 21,760 in 1947. This reflected the use of more powerful locomotives, and it meant that fewer freight cars were needed. There were about 2,610,000 freight cars in the United States at the end of the 1920s, declining to about 2,025,000 in 1947, even though the tonnage was virtually unchanged and the average distance of shipment considerably higher in 1947.

In Britain the picture was somewhat different, with freight tonnage declining from about 330 million in 1929 to 275 million in 1955. This situation of declining freight traffic was typical of many European countries and would soon threaten others. Only in the communist world, where there was a deliberate neglect of highway transportation, was freight traffic inexorably rising. But this brought its own problems, in the form of remarkably inefficient railroads.

Below: A local freight train comes down from the Scottish Highlands into Inverness. Empty open cars, used for domestic coal, form part of the train, which is hauled by an elderly locomotive originally built by the former Caledonian Railway for passenger service. The picture dates from the mid-1950s.

Opposite, above: An old box car awaiting restoration. This is a wooden-bodied vehicle with metal ends and metal frames. The automatic coupler is visible; the rod leading from it, with its bent hand-grip, is to enable yard staff to open the jaws for coupling up without stepping between the cars.

Opposite, below: The same car, showing the standard truck that evolved in the U.S. after the 1850s. Its square journal boxes have hinged lids for the replenishment of lubricant, originally grease, later oil-soaked cotton waste. Lubricant failure could produce "hot boxes," which in bad cases caused melting and train derailment, or fire, or sometimes both.

Above: Different railroads designed different cabooses. This Union Pacific example is notable for its high cupola from which the rear-end brakeman or conductor observed the train, watching in particular for the wisp of smoke that was the first sign of a hot box.

Opposite: A local freight in central Wales. Long single-track lines were rare in Britain, and were found mainly in rural areas of Wales and Scotland where traffic was sparse. This short freight train, and two or three passenger trains, would have been the entire day's work for this line in the early 1950s, when this picture was taken.

Below: A milk tank car used in overnight service from western England into London. Normally, milk trains were hauled by a passenger locomotive, not the freight locomotive shown here. The latter is of the 2-8-0 type introduced by the Great Western Railway in 1903 and incorporating U.S. features. Only two decades separate this design from the GWR's former standard freight locomotive, the six-wheeler in the picture opposite.

Above: Narrow- (3ft-) gauge railroads were common in Colorado and some still exist as tourist lines. At one time, they were the only means of freight transport for mining communities. This picture shows a typical collection of rolling stock at the now defunct station of Gunnison. The water tower is well insulated against the cold winters of this mountainous terrain.

Opposite: A cattle-loading ramp, now a museum piece near Albany, Texas. Driving animals into freight cars was not always a tranquil job, but as soon as one was in, the rest would usually follow.

Overleaf, page 140, above: The 2-6-0 was soon superseded by the 2-8-0 for heavy freight work. This 2-8-0 of the Boston & Albany RR was supplied in the 1890s and has the small driving wheels required when tractive effort is more important than speed.

Page 140, below: Rail-water interchange was common, especially in America and Russia, taking the form of station quays where freight and passengers were transhipped or, quite often, where the freight cars were themselves carried on ferries. This is the scene at Wilson's Point, near Norwalk, Connecticut, whence the ferry served Oyster Bay, Long Island.

Page 141: The ornate façade of the Hudson River RR's freight terminal in New York City. Loading/unloading tracks were on ground level, with the upper floors used mainly for storage.

Opposite, above: Small-scale freight: a wayside freight station on a Colorado narrow-gauge railroad.

Opposite, below: Large-scale freight: the busy freight yard at Port Waratah, New South Wales, in 1971. Locomotives like the 2-8-0 in the foreground brought in export coal destined for the quayside. In the middle distance are the storage tracks, and the harbor cranes can be seen in the background. Other coal trains await their turn on the storage tracks.

Below: Highway competition hardly existed in communist countries, as is suggested by this empty road paralleling a main railway route in Hungary. The freight train is hauled by one of the well-known 424-Class 4-8-0 locomotives.

Right: Small locomotive, small freight cars; a train of coal empties on British Railways in the 1950s. This class of six-wheel locomotive originated on the Midland Railway in 1911 and was built for three decades, even though it was really too small for the job.

Opposite, below: The last German coal company to use steam yard locomotives, at Aachen in the 1980s. The tank locomotive is a standard German eight-wheeler, designed for industrial use.

Below: A German-built 2-6-0 hauls a train of locally mined coal at Concepción in Chile.

Overleaf: A mixed freight crossing the Chaumont Viaduct in eastern France. The locomotive is of the final class of French Railways 2-10-0 heavy-haulage units, built from 1939 to 1951. They were 4-cylinder compounds, with mechanical stokers.

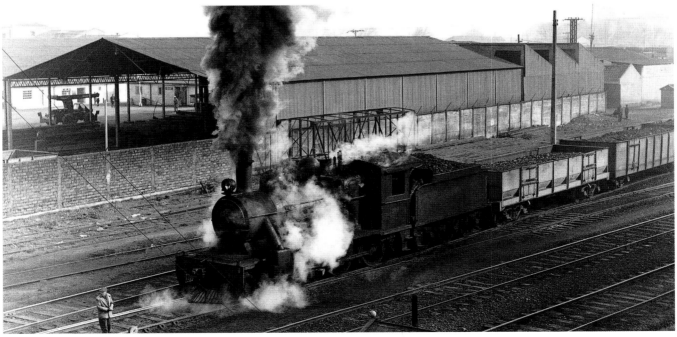

Below: By the end of the twentieth century, heavy steam-freight operation could be witnessed only in China. This is part of the classification yard at Dalien.

Opposite, above: An old-style sorting yard at Swansea Docks in South Wales. The shunter, complete with his shunting pole, can just be discerned at left.

Opposite, below: A big modern classification yard at Kharbin, China. Cars are pushed over a hump (behind the photographer), and then roll by gravity over retarders (in middle foreground) which adjust their speed so that they stop gently in the train assembly track into which they are directed (background).

Previous pages, above: A Spanish freight train approaches Zaragoza behind a 2-8-2 locomotive. The third vehicle has a brakeman's shelter, a once-common feature of European freight trains but already archaic when this picture was made in the 1970s.

Previous pages, below: Local freight in South Africa. A 4-8-0 locomotive, once a mainline freight machine, potters about the yard at Oudtshoorn.

Above: A sheep-carrying car of the Denver & Rio Grande RR. Livestock cars had slatted sides for ventilation, and sheep cars usually had two, sometimes three, floors. Although animal transportation in the nineteenth century developed quickly, it was difficult traffic because trains had to stop at regular intervals for feeding and watering.

Opposite, above: A refrigerator car of the Pacific Fruit Express company. These cars had ice compartments, replenished through the roof.

Opposite, below: Many freight car inscriptions have long since disappeared, and others were rare from the start. The Saltair Route was a name adopted by the short Heber Valley RR in Utah.

Overleaf, pages 154–55: A freight "extra" leaves North Bay in Ontario, hauled by a Canadian Pacific 4-6-2.

Page 155, above: A Canadian National six-wheel switcher sorts cars at Bonaventure Yard, in the center of the busy city of Montreal.

Page 155, below, right: One of the Canadian National's biggest freight locomotives, a 2-10-2, hauls a heavy train into Winnipeg, Manitoba.

Engineering
and Architecture

Railroad builders had a choice of approach. They could build lines that would stand the test of decades, with solid structures, easy grades, and smooth curves, or they could lay their tracks cheaply in the expectation of improving them as increasing traffic brought both the need and the money to do so. Which choice was made depended on how much money was available and how much traffic was initially expected, so usually it was lines in long-existing economies, serving well-populated points, that had the benefit of costly engineering, while countries that were still being developed, where the railroad was a means rather than a result of development, found themselves with rough-and-ready lines.

Some of the early European railways, like the Great Western in Britain and the St Petersburg–Moscow in Russia, were built so solidly that even today their structures are still carrying trains of speeds and weights undreamed-of when they were first built. But the cheap railroad was not without its advantages, quite apart from enabling lines to be built that simply could not have been financed if standards had been higher. The long process of improvement after traffic developed meant that early decisions were not binding over the long term. Although

the London & Birmingham Railway, for example, had some magnificent structures, including one very costly tunnel to avoid a steep grade, the dimensions of its rolling stock were forever limited. The width and height of British rolling stock remained considerably smaller than American and even smaller than the narrow-gauge South African railways. The width restriction, in particular, hampered the final development of the British steam locomotive because it placed a limit on the size of cylinders that could be used; British locomotives were limited to a 9ft width, but the U.S. limit was 10ft 9in, and the 3ft 6in gauge South African lines could take 10 feet.

A few early American lines followed the British example of solid construction; the Baltimore & Ohio RR in the 1830s built the durable eight-arch stone viaduct across the Patapsco River in Maryland,

Opposite: Grand Central Terminal, New York City, once the starting point for famous trains like the "Twentieth Century Limited," deploys still record numbers of commuter trains. Seen here is the main concourse, as restored in the 1990s. The 125ft-high vaulted ceiling has an astronomical theme in which sixty of the largest stars are highlighted by bright electric lights.

Below: Seashells used as track ballast in the New Orleans area.

Right: The masonry viaduct at Chaumont in eastern France. It was built by the Est Railway to carry both Paris-to-Switzerland main line trains and north-south trains between Reims and Dijon. Although not a true double-deck structure, it was designed with some ingenuity to provide a walkway as well.

and also a stone arch bridge at Mount Clare in Baltimore that was destined to remain the oldest U.S. railroad bridge. The still-standing Starucca Viaduct is another example of solid construction; it was built by the Erie Railroad, which adopted high standards from the start. But the typical practice was to build elementary wooden bridges or viaducts and lay rails on freshly-cut crossties, managing without rock ballast. Where possible the lines followed the contours of the land, with heights conquered by winding alignments that were longer but cheaper than tunnels. In course of time timber viaducts and bridges would be replaced by iron or steel structures, and some mountain lines might be shortened with the construction of a few tunnels, but the latter was an expensive solution and was not often attempted. When traffic became heavy and speeds increased, heavier rails on rectangular, creosoted crossties, which were generally held firm by rock ballast, steadily replaced the accident-prone and hard-to-maintain original track.

Sometimes tunnels were unavoidable. The transcontinental lines through the Rockies had to resort to combinations of both tunnelling and spiralling, resulting in a number of spiral tunnels. The longest steam-operated tunnel in North America was located in the Rockies, being the 1927 Moffat Tunnel near Denver in Colorado, which was over six miles long.

Both in America and Europe the experience of the previous generation's canal-builders was available and in Britain, especially, the tall long viaducts over river valleys followed canal-engineering practice. But there were advances. The curved viaduct (really a succession of straight spans placed in a curved alignment) was sometimes used, and the Great Western Railway's Maidenhead Viaduct frightened contemporaries with a series of arches that were so flat that they seemed unlikely to stand the weight of a train (but they did, and still do).

In France high masonry viaducts were just as common as in Great Britain, and equally long-lasting. But in Alexandre

Eiffel France produced an engineer who knew how to exploit the steel girder; Eiffel's most significant legacy is not the Eiffel Tower but a series of transportation structures that he designed for France and other countries.

With the advent of steel construction came the crossing of wide rivers and estuaries; almost every country had its great structure. Scotland's Tay Bridge came to grief disastrously in a storm, but the huge cantilever Forth Bridge, built in 1890 and measuring 8,298 feet, carried the double-track North British Railway from Edinburgh toward the Highlands. In India there were wide rivers that had the habit of changing their courses, giving rise to a series of long steel viaducts that seemed to be three or four times longer than was necessary. Australia had its Hawkesbury River Bridge and, comparatively late in the steam era, the 1932 combined road and rail Sydney Harbour Bridge, which had the world's largest steel arch span (of 1,650 feet). The world's largest cantilever span was over the St. Lawrence at Quebec, the main span being 1,800 feet. Finished in 1917, its construction had a suggestion of trial and error about it; a 1907 attempt went down with seventy-five lives and the final 1917 construction was achieved only after another lethal collapse.

Of the very long railroad bridges, that crossing the St. Lawrence at Montreal was the earliest, being a tubular structure designed by Robert Stephenson and measuring, with approaches, almost two miles. It was built in 1859 but was replaced forty years later. For some years the 1917 Hell Gate Bridge of the Pennsylvania RR at New York was the world's second-longest railway bridge at 19,233 feet. It was surpassed only by the 878 brick arches supporting the London & Greenwich Railway over London's rooftops, opened in 1836. But in 1935 the Huey P. Long Bridge was opened at New

Below: The Quebec Bridge across the St. Lawrence River. Costly in both lives and money, this long cantilever structure, built by the Canadian government, never carried the high volume of rail traffic that was anticipated.

Opposite, above: The western terminal of the Canadian Pacific at Vancouver, British Columbia. This Neoclassical façade was more imposing than the tracks behind it, which never carried a dense service.

Opposite, below: The 1915 depot of the Milwaukee Railroad at Great Falls, Montana. This was not on the main line, and in the last decades of steam saw only freight trains.

Orleans, totalling 23,235 feet, and this was destined to remain the world's longest railway bridge of the steam era.

The United States was also the site of the world's longest water crossings. First came the Lucin Cut-off of 1904, which was a 20-mile timber trestle, gradually replaced by an embankment, across the expanse of the Great Salt Lake in Utah. The combination of bridges and embankments that jumped from islet to islet to form the 128-mile Key West Extension of the Florida East Coast RR had only a short life, being completed in 1912 and demolished by a hurricane in 1935.

In the late nineteenth century steel rails replaced iron, and were harder wearing and less liable to fracture. In the early years many different rail types had been tried, but finally two prevailed. These were the flat-bottom rail, which was held to the tie ("sleeper" in Britain) by spikes, and the bullhead, which was laid in chairs that were bolted to the ties. Bullhead looked more elaborate and may have been somewhat more resistant to lateral thrusts, but was more expensive to maintain, partly because the wedges holding

the rail in each chair tended to drop out periodically; all British tracks were patrolled daily by a lengthman carrying a long-handled hammer. In general, British railways used the bullhead rail and other countries, the flat-bottom, although at the end of the steam era British railways were beginning the shift over to the flat-bottom type.

Although pioneer lines might have ties laid directly on the prepared ground, some form of ballasting was really essential. Ballast performed several functions. It drained the top surface, it provided a firm base for the track, necessary to ensure long wear and reduce breakages, and it anchored the track so that it did not creep out of alignment under the passage of successive trains. The best ballast was granite stone of a certain size, but not all railroads could obtain this. Sometimes gravel or sand was used instead. Seashells, where they were obtainable, made excellent ballast, and in Soviet Russia great use was made of asbestos waste.

The earliest passenger stations were simply developments of coaching practice, tickets typically being sold at a

Right: A Californian Spanish-Mission style depot of the Santa Fe Railway, built in 1927 near San Diego, at Riverside, which also had depots of the Southern Pacific and Union Pacific Railroads. In addition to these three, North America had forty-eight other depots named Riverside in the 1950s.

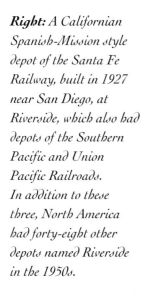

nearby inn and trains boarded from track level. Gradually covered accommodation was provided and, in most countries, a semblance of a platform. In Britain the high platform, just below the level of the train's floor, was provided, but in other countries the low platform was favored. The first terminal depots, like those in Liverpool and Baltimore, at first provided only a single platform.

The railroad passenger depot was never a specific architectural form. It followed the technical requirements of its time, while its style reflected contemporary fashions. Newly built main lines tended to have a unifying style. The Brighton Line in Britain was notable for its Italianate station buildings, complete with campanile in some cases. The Great Central had a standard design of main station, including a single island (double-sided) platform reached by stairs from an overhead highway bridge. In Russia's bureaucratic empire, depots were categorized according to their importance, and a standard design imposed for each category. In another bureaucratic empire, India, the pattern was different, with an attempt being made to merge British practice with local tradition. With the 1857 Indian Mutiny in mind, the British provided cities with a central terminal whose architecture might include defensive features like slitted walls, and an out-of-town cantonment station for the use of British officials and troops. In other parts of the British Empire, and also in Argentina, which was strongly influenced by Britain and her empire, quite imposing city terminals were built, following British practice of the time. In North America, too, there was a period when city authorities gloried in magnificent terminals; these often had a classical frontage

Above: *The original New York Central Railroad train shed at Manhattan's Grand Central Depot (1871), on 42nd Street. The railroad soon outgrew this facility, and the new Grand Central Terminal of 1913 solved traffic problems with electrified underground tracks on two levels.*

To protect passengers from the elements the all-over roof had been adopted. So long as wood was the material the span of such roofs was limited, but when iron, and later steel, appeared, it was possible to span many tracks with a single arched roof. The Midland Railway's St. Pancras Station of 1868 in London had a span of 240 feet, but this was eclipsed in 1892 by a newly built Broad Street Station in Philadelphia, with a 300-foot span.

But in time the high cost of maintaining these metal spans led to a reversion to simple awnings over the individual platforms. A landmark of the new architecture was the Helsinki terminal in Finland, which had a modest frontage and practically no protection over the platforms. In the Interwar dictatorships there was a return to pomp and grandeur. In the Soviet Union, Stalin's taste for the grandiose was manifested notably in the stations of the new Moscow Metro. Mussolini made his mark with Milan Central, which appeared to be trying to outmatch Milan Cathedral and which presented the unfortunate passenger with great staircases and an imposing, but irksome, stretch of distance between entrance and platforms.

In America the grandest terminal of all, New York City's Grand Central, was not designed for steam trains. With platforms at two levels it was the world's largest station on many counts (but it was not the busiest or the longest; Clapham Junction in London handled around 2,000 trains daily, or four times more than Grand Central, and Khargpur station in India had a 3,500-foot platform). The 1907 Beaux-Arts style Washington Union Station (thirty-two platforms against Grand Central's forty-four) was the largest U.S. station used by steam trains.

and sometimes a tower (the higher the better; Chicago Grand Central's tower of 1890 soared to 249 feet).

Changing fashions ensured that there would always be variety in railroad architecture. The Gothic Revival in England resulted notably in the "Red-Brick Gothic" of St. Pancras Station, but there was also a Slavic Revival in Russia that produced among other curiosities the frontage of the Rizhskii Station in Moscow. Also, railway companies often tried to adopt local architectural traditions in their buildings. In the American West, Spanish forms were utilized in, among others, the Los Angeles and Albuquerque stations. In Britain it was possible to find stations that looked like churches, castles, and baronial halls.

Growing traffic meant that larger city terminals were needed in the late nineteenth century. Big depots consisted of two elements, the platform area and the terminal building. The latter became a huge block, designed to impress and frequently including a grand railway-owned hotel. The platform area was more of an engineering than architectural problem.

The smaller stations passed through fewer fashions and for the most part preserved a certain small-scale charm lacking in the big city terminals. In the early years there was a definite tendency to make the small station fit modestly into its surroundings, perhaps in a subconscious endeavor to make clients feel at home. Some station buildings resembled cottages, others town houses, but they provided the same services of ticket office, baggage and parcels offices, and facilities for waiting passengers. This modest style predominated throughout the steam era, even though there were later stations that tried to keep in step with prevailing architectural fashions, the use of concrete being one such fashion. Most local stations have never been rebuilt, apart from those involved in wars. The Trans Siberian line still has its ornate stations with local-style decoration disguising the "official" architecture underneath. In Britain the different fretwork patterns of the awning valances distinguish the stations of one former company from another.

In Europe stone and brick were the usual materials for small stations, while in the Americas wood was most common. The wooden way-station, with its arched roof, was encountered all over North America, basically the same everywhere but with local differentiations that nowadays delight architectural historians. Such stations usually provided accommodation for the agent and often for an operator-telegraphist who would hand train orders up to passing locomotive men. Platform awnings were rare, unlike in Europe, and any platform was rudimentary and unlikely to be paved. Some were flag-stops, with trains halting only if a flag was displayed.

***Below:** Cannon Street Station, the London terminus of the South Eastern & Chatham Railway, about 1900. This station still serves the southern commuter lines. Both towers remain, but the roof has been replaced.*

Page 164: With so many navigable waterways crossed by the railroads, lift bridges and swing bridges were quite common in North America. This bridge is at Plaquemine, Louisiana, where the Texas & Pacific Railroad crossed a branch of the Mississippi.

Page 165, above: A Southern Pacific 4-8-4 locomotive crosses an arch-truss bridge at Tobin, California.

Page 165, below: An elementary trestle bridge at Georgetown, Colorado. This is a narrow-gauge line near Denver, part of which has been preserved in operation.

Opposite, above: Iron or steel girders on masonry piles formed one of the simplest, most economical, and most common ways of crossing water. This typical example was at Guardbridge in eastern Scotland, where the North British Railway passed over a tidal inlet.

Below: The curved masonry viaduct that still carries the railway tracks over the rooftops of Brighton, in southern England, into the terminus. This picture dates from the 1950s.

Opposite, above: A Bangkok-bound train crosses a simple wooden trestle bridge in southern Thailand. Made from local teak, this structure easily bears the 60-ton weight of the Japanese-built locomotive.

Opposite, below: Bridging the Susquehanna River at Perryville, Maryland. Once part of the Pennsylvania Railroad main line, although built for the Philadelphia, Baltimore & Washington Railroad, the bridge rests on masonry piers designed to cope with heavy storm flows and floating ice.

Above: Less numerous than stations, locomotive depots were still common features of the railroad landscape. In the United States they were usually roundhouses, with locomotive stalls fanning out from a central turntable. They were often dark, cramped, and plain because companies saw no reason for extravagance in buildings that the public did not visit. This is a roundhouse-type depot at Savannah, Georgia.

Opposite, above: Seemingly supported on mere beanpoles, an Atlantic & Pacific Railroad train crosses the insubstantial-looking trestle bridge over the Pecos River at Canyon Diablo, Arizona. This 1880s route through the state later became part of the Santa Fe Railway's main line.

Below: An interesting arch-bridge design, dispensing with the usual fill-in masonry between the vertical supports. It carried the Richmond, Fredericksburg & Potomac Railroad over the James River at Richmond, Virginia. The picture dates from 1900; the train was probably stationary, the high-velocity "exhaust" being air-brushed in later.

Opposite: Water tower design differed from railroad to railroad. This example still serves its original purpose, being located on the New Mexico/Colorado narrow-gauge line that later became the Cumbres & Toltec tourist railroad.

Below: Very occasionally, locomotive depots had an individual as well as a utilitarian style. The builders of this long-disused example of a roundhouse in Colorado made use of the local stone to produce a structure that is plainly craftsman-built.

Overleaf, page 174: Building the Canadian Pacific in 1883. This is one of the gangs employed by the contractor Onderdonck, building eastward from Vancouver; the location is British Columbia's Fraser River Valley.

Page 175, above: A train enters Flax Bourton Tunnel in Somerset, southern England. Early tunnels through rock were usually left unlined, but had brick portals (to reassure fearful passengers, it was said). This tunnel was originally built to accommodate the Great Western Railway's 7ft-gauge tracks, which explains the wide clearances.

Page 175, below: One of several tunnels on the Canadian Pacific line through the Rockies, south of Kamloops Lake.

Opposite, above: For years the U.S. capital had dingy railroad facilities, but in 1907 the Washington Union Terminal was built to accommodate trains of the several railroads serving the city. The Beaux-Arts style façade, recently refurbished, is largely unchanged.

Opposite, below: One of the many embellishments of the Grand Central Terminal in New York City, viewed here from 42nd Street. Above the grand three-bay façade, Mercury, the messenger of the gods, presides over a sculptural group.

Overleaf, page 178: Classical styling at its height: the Roman baths at Caracalla were the architect's model for the main concourse of New York City's Pennsylvania Station. Built in 1910, this landmark had a short life; it was pulled down in 1963.

Below: A view of the imposing Italian Renaissance-style façade and roofline cornice of the Reading Railroad's terminal in Philadelphia, built in 1893. The terminal was ornamented with terra-cotta and originally featured a copper roof balustrade.

UNION STATION
PENNSYLVANIA R.R. | BURLINGTON ROUTE | THE ALTON ROAD | MILWAUKEE R.R.

nion Station CHICAGO, ILL.
C-5

Page 179, above: Union Station in Chicago, completed after World War I. It was used by only some of the big railroads serving the city, although nowadays it is the Amtrak terminal.

Page 179, below: The 1914 Baltimore Union Station, like Chicago Union, was of Neoclassical style. Like Chicago, it too is now an Amtrak station. Apart from electrification, it remains largely unchanged.

Left: Toledo Station in Spain was built in traditional Spanish style with Moorish ornamentation. This is the booking hall.

Opposite: The Canadian National station at Arundel, north of Montreal, converted for use as a post office.

Below: Settle Station on the Midland Railway's Settle and Carlisle line in northern England, which created a third London-to-Scotland route in the 1870s.

Below: The massive Doric arch fronting the Euston terminus of the London & Birmingham Railway in London. A similar but smaller arch was placed at the other terminus in Birmingham. This was a pioneer intercity railway, and the arches asserted the dignity and solidity of the new technology. The Euston Arch was pulled down in the 1960s, when the terminal was rebuilt, and the recriminations have not yet ceased.

Opposite, above: The Gare du Nord, Paris. The scene of many celebrated events, both real and fictional, this station was built by France's Northern Railway. During the steam age, it was the terminus of, among other famous lines, the London-Paris Golden Arrow and the Nord Express to Scandinavia.

Opposite, below: Leipzig was Germany's biggest rail station. The trains were sandwiched between two platforms, one for passenger use and the other for baggage and parcel trolleys. The picture dates from 1975, when the German Democratic Republic was still using steam traction.

Previous pages: The Spanish-Mission-style complex at Caliente, Nevada (1923), which serviced Union Pacific equipment and included two restaurants and a hotel.

Opposite: The Rizhskii (Riga) terminus in Moscow, an example of the early twentieth-century Slavic Revival, or Neo-Slavic, style. In Moscow and St. Petersburg, city terminals took the name of the main destination they served (which is why, for example, Moscow Station is in St. Petersburg and St. Petersburg Station is in Moscow).

Below: In Bombay, this grandiose administrative block was added to the existing station in 1887 to create the Victoria Terminus of the Great Indian Peninsula Railway. The style, which was officially termed "Gothic-Saracenic," blended the British Gothic Revival and Indian themes.

Above: Vladivostok, the Pacific terminal of the Trans Siberian Railway. Built in the early twentieth century, it incorporates Neo-Slavic features. Although recently refurbished, this station has not been greatly altered, although the trains are faster now. In 1914 the fastest train to Moscow took nine days.

Left: In Soviet times, not every Russian main station had a statue of Lenin or Stalin, but many did. What was obligatory was the display of at least one official portrait inside station buildings; some of them are still in place.

Below: A postcard view of Lime Street Station in Liverpool, northwestern England, dating from the early twentieth century. This was not the terminus of the Liverpool & Manchester Railway, but of the London & North Western, which liked to style itself the "Premier Line." At that time Liverpool, a main seaport for goods and passengers to the Americas and elsewhere, was a lucrative traffic center for the L&NWR, and its impressive station reflected that fact.

Lime Street, Liverpool

Opposite, above: Cheyenne, Wyoming, was another important place on the Union Pacific line. It was a locomotive-changing point, and marked the beginning of the long climb toward the Rockies. The depot shown here was built of Colorado sandstone in 1887, its architects incorporating Romanesque features.

Opposite, below: An 1899 photograph of the Canadian Pacific Station at Lethbridge, Alberta. The dual gauge was to accommodate narrow-gauge trains serving a local coal company.

Below: Union Station in Omaha, Nebraska. Omaha was the starting point for the transcontinental Union Pacific Railroad and therefore became (and remained) its headquarters city. The depot pictured here was built in 1870, when traffic was increasing, and was not replaced until the 1930s.

Overleaf: The grand "Casa del Desierto" complex at Barstow, California. It was built by the Santa Fe Railway in 1911 to accommodate a hotel, a Harvey House restaurant, and station offices.

Railroad People

The steam-era railroader was different from other workers and knew it. He felt he belonged to a community of workers who relied on him just as he relied on them. He had a sense of hierarchy, although this was less marked in America than in Europe, where there had been quasi-military organization on the early steam railways. Precisely defined ranks, and uniforms, led to divisions within the community. Everywhere, the enginemen regarded themselves as an elite, and they were treated as such, not least in the matter of their pay.

As for railwaywomen, these were rare among operating workers in peacetime. But the railroad wife was certainly part of the railway community, and suffered from the irregular work shifts. If her husband worked with the freight trains, she would never be sure when he would get back home. Some railway families went as long as ten years without spending Christmas, for example, or Thanksgiving holidays together.

Railroad staff could be divided broadly into operating and non-operating. Most office workers fell into the second group and the first was filled mainly by enginemen (drivers, firemen, locomotive maintenance workers), train crew (conductors or guards, brakemen, as well as sleeping car porters or attendants), station personnel (inspectors, freight and passenger porters, switchmen, station agents or station masters, freight yard personnel), and those who controlled the movement of the trains, including despatchers and their local operators in North America, and the signalmen throwing their levers in the signal boxes and control towers of British and other railway routes.

Opposite: Women take over "men's work" in World War II. Here, in a 1943 news picture, female locomotive cleaners get to work on a Southern Pacific passenger locomotive at the Bakersfield depot in California.

Left: A British locomotive man in characteristic pose, oiling up the sliding surfaces at the crosshead.

Above: The smokebox door had to be opened daily, to clear away accumulated soot. After this dirty job was done, each clip was tightened hard, to prevent air leaks.

The conductor, known as the guard in most of the British Empire, was in effect the train's captain, responsible for its good running and for making decisions in emergencies. On most railways he kept a journal in which delays were entered, together with their causes. The conductor of a passenger train had an air of gold-braided distinction and was meant to be exemplary in his dignity. In America he would have risen from a boy's job to brakeman and trainman before being promoted to freight-train conductor. British guards, too, spent years as freight-train guards. Whereas the American freight conductor would have his caboose, in which he could sleep and prepare meals as well as attend to his paperwork, the British

guard had simply his austere brake van, also at the end of the train, that could oscillate madly and unexpectedly. A good performance with freight trains, seniority, and a suitable vacancy might enable the crude life of the freight guard or conductor to be exchanged for the gentlemanly, brass-buttoned life of a passenger conductor.

In the early days, railroads expanded faster than the supply of competent locomotive crews, so the latter were prized and well-rewarded. In later periods, when traffic fell, they were rarely dismissed, although they might find themselves with fewer turns to work. Regarding themselves as an elite, they were never keen to join a general railway trade union or brotherhood, but preferred to organize their own. In North America, where locomotive drivers were called engineers as a mark of their technical competence and status, the locomotive men's brotherhood was sometimes bitterly at odds with the other railroad brotherhoods. In Britain, too, the enginemen's trade union was frequently out of step with the other railway unions. In North America the career route of a locomotive man was less fixed than elsewhere. A man might start out as a call-boy, then veer off to become a brakeman, and eventually find his way onto the footplate. Those who arrived there after starting their career as a fitter in a locomotive depot had a certain professional advantage, as did those who knew what it was like to be a conductor or depot agent. In North America, although a growing number of lines were equipped with block signaling, most lines were single-track and operated by the train-order system, which placed extra responsibility on enginemen. The train order gave them precise instructions as to their schedule and where they should take siding to let other trains pass. Any mistakes could be fatal, which is why engineer and fireman were required to read the train order out aloud to each other to ensure that it was understood. Passing intermediate stations, the engine crew might pick up from the depot's agent or operator amended train orders telegraphed by the distant train despatcher, and the same routine was followed. Compared to locomotive men in other countries, who were guided by a succession of visual line-side signals, the American engineer seemed to carry a more lonesome responsibility.

In Britain and her empire a young man would expect to pass through set stages: he would start as a cleaner, progress to fireman, and then become a driver. Within the last two stages there would be subdivisions, the aspirant beginning with yard locomotives, then moving to local freight trains, long-distance freight trains, then passenger trains, beginning with slow passenger trains, and ending his career, if he was lucky, as a "top-link" driver with the best locomotives on the fastest trains. Luck entered the picture by making speed of promotion depend on vacancies. If the locality or the period were stagnant, few vacancies would occur and a good man could end his career still as fireman. On the other hand, in periods of traffic growth a man might whisk through the stages and become a driver in late youth. In Australia, which followed British practice, the future prime minister Joseph Chifley was one of the lucky ones, joining the railways in 1903 as a shop boy and progressing rapidly

through positions as a cleaner, acting fireman, fireman, and acting driver to full driver status in 1914.

A feature of the British system was that it involved no formal learning. Voluntary classes were usually available, but were not compulsory; all learning was on the job, mainly by observing the work of seniors. But there was an oral examination at the entry to fireman and driver stages, which was rigorous in its testing of the aspirant's knowledge of the rule book. Under the British system, speed of promotion did not depend on whether a candidate was a good or merely a mediocre worker.

Below: One of the lesser chores of a locomotive depot, refilling the sand dome. The vital requirement here was to ensure that the sand remained absolutely dry.

Above: Locomotive men at Capetown, South Africa, in the 1970s. At that period of apartheid, the higher locomotive grades were reserved for white passengers.

Right: One of the last steam locomotive crews in Australia; the driver (left) and fireman of a yard locomotive at Sydney Harbour.

Very different was French practice, where aspirant drivers were required to study the theoretical as well as the practical side of their profession. French locomotive designers developed complex locomotives, like the compounds with their choice of driving modes, in the belief that the drivers would understand how to get the best out of them. Elsewhere in continental Europe future drivers received theoretical training at polytechnics or special institutes.

In most countries railroad staff were expected to know by heart their companies' rule books, which laid down quite unambiguously how each operation, and each emergency, should be handled. In North America, on most railroads, this was called the Operating Rules, in Britain, the Rule Book, and in most of the continental European countries, the Technical Rules. Safety of train operations could be ensured only if each employee acted in the prescribed manner. But there were also some non-operating matters that were made clear. A typical nineteenth-century British company rule book prescribed that: "Every

person is to come on duty daily, clean in his person and clothes, shaved, and his shoes blacked"; and "It is urgently requested every person…on Sundays and Holy Days, when he is not required on duty, that he will attend a place of worship; as it will be the means of promotion when vacancies occur." In North America, throughout the steam age and beyond, the first pages of the Operating Rules were occupied by general homilies of which perhaps the most often cited was Rule G: "The use of intoxicants by employees while on duty is prohibited. Their use, or the frequenting of places where they are sold, is sufficient cause for dismissal."

Violations of Rule G were the most frequent cause of dismissal on some lines. In the United States, however, it was quite common for a dismissed employee to find a new position with another company or even, after a decent interval, with his old company.

In the railroads' disciplined organization, any failure to obey orders, or to turn up for work at the right time, could mean dismissal. But so, depending on time and place, could a host of other things, like that authoritarian catch-all, "levity." Loss of free pass privileges or docked pay was a sanction for minor violations. In the first decades of the twentieth century some American companies introduced a more predictable system, in which merit and demerit points were awarded to individuals. Sixty demerits could warrant dismissal in most schemes. The name of the New York Central RR superintendent who devised the scheme was Brown, so merits soon became known as "Brownie points." But dismissals remained high.

In the last decade of the steam railway in Canada, for example, the Canadian National was dismissing about a thousand workers annually, although almost half of them somehow managed to get themselves reinstated.

Although railroad staff had unique opportunities for pilferage, most railway crime was committed by outsiders. Robbery with violence ranged from assaults on individual passengers to assaults on entire trains; the train hold-up was most common in the United States, but other countries had similar experiences. The bandits sometimes enjoyed public sympathy, not only because they had a romantic "Robin Hood" air about them, but because the public did not love the railroads, which were widely seen as arrogant monopolies. In America the Pinkerton detective agency prospered as a result of offering its services to the railroads, and in due course most railways organized their own police forces. In some, including Russia and India, uniformed armed guards traveled with high-value freight, a practice that continued beyond the

Left: World War I brought many European women into railway jobs previously the exclusive territory of men. This is one of the first female ticket collectors in Britain.

Below: The driver of a British Railways tank locomotive takes things easy between station stops.

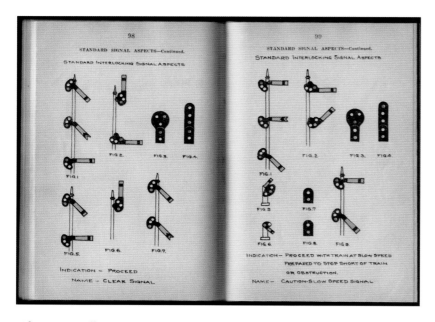

Above: *Not all was text in North American railroad rule books. Signal indications were spread over several pages. This is a Long Island Railroad book of 1926, but all companies followed the same pattern.*

steam age. In Britain the company police forces eventually became the Transport Police; it had all the appearances of the ordinary police force, but was outside the control of local authorities. In post-Independence India the railways had not only their uniformed, armed Railway Protection Force, but also a secret police organization.

In the nineteenth century the life expectancy of a railwayman was on a par with that of a deep-sea fisherman. Working beside moving machinery, a man could suffer death or maiming from a simple stumble or lapse of concentration. In North America, the most dangerous work was that of switchmen and freight-train brakemen in the pre-automatic brake, pre-automatic coupler days. They coupled and uncoupled by deftly dropping or pulling a pin while the cars were in motion. An unlucky or inattentive man could progressively lose one finger after another in this job, and the more fingers he lost, the more likely he was to lose an entire arm or his life in the next miscalculation. Even if he survived the couplers, a brakeman could

still be blown or shaken off a train roof as he ran backward and forward to apply the hand brakes.

In the decade before 1914, annual casualty rates on Britain's railways averaged around 500 deaths and almost 25,000 recorded injuries. The greatest number of casualties was suffered by track maintenance workers, but the trade with the lowest expectation of life was probably that of the shunter; British freight cars were coupled with loose chains, and the yard shunter ran alongside the moving vehicles, hooking and unhooking the chains with his long pole. Dark nights, fog, and ice took their toll.

Railroad owners and managers did deplore the loss of life, especially of scarce skilled men. In pre-insurance days they would try to raise money for bereaved families and often made donations themselves. Better still, they would find jobs for widows and bereaved children; on French railway stations foreign males are still embarrassed by the presence of women attendants in men's toilets, a practice that arose to provide jobs for railway widows (the luckier ones became crossing keepers). But when money was needed to improve safety, the railway owners were no better than other contemporary industrialists. In Britain the struggle they put up against government attempts to impose automatic brakes was something of an epic, and U.S. railroads did not hurry to fit the Westinghouse brake.

By the end of the nineteenth century, railway trade unions were taking hold, but in most countries it was public opinion that persuaded railway managements that working conditions for their personnel needed to be improved, if only to reduce the accident rate.

The railway trade unions of Europe and the brotherhoods of North America had their big strikes; the Pullman strike of 1894, protesting against wage cuts, was a failure because local agitators forced the issue and started a strike before the brotherhood (this was a young general railway union) was strong enough to fight. Moreover, governments in America, just as in Russia, were prepared to send in troops against strikers. In Britain there were general railway strikes in 1911, 1919, and 1926, which for the most part were failures. The British strikes were less violent than those in America, even though the companies could if necessary call upon the forces of law and order. The Taff Vale Railway strike, involving a small Welsh colliery line, led to the "Taff Vale Case," in which the court decided that the trade union, which had announced a strike to force the company to grant it official recognition, was liable to pay damages to the railway company. This case set a precedent that crippled British trade unions—and not just the railway unions—for some years.

But although all over the world most strikes seemed to meet defeat, they certainly made railroad managements more careful, more willing to make concessions. U.S. railroads even agreed that freight-train crews should remain practically unchanged despite automatic couplers and automatic brakes; hence by the 1950s the railroads were the supreme example of "featherbedding." Moreover, North American train and locomotive crews extracted wage rates based on a "day" of 100 miles, and this remained unchanged when faster trains enabled crews to cover that distance in three hours. High wage bills encouraged the railroads to operate heavier, and therefore fewer, trains, which in the interwar years resulted in the introduction of ever-larger locomotives.

A product of the Railway Age was the railway town, which existed solely to serve the steam railway. In large countries including Canada, the United States, and Russia, division points, where locomotives were changed and freight trains inspected, were established. These were often in the wilds and developed into towns. When the steam locomotive was replaced by the diesel, which could run for hundreds of miles without change, many division points were closed down, sometimes condemning an entire community to unemployment and purposelessness. Such a situation was rare in Britain. Towns that grew from nothing to centers of locomotive work like Swindon and Ashford diversified so much that by the time steam-locomotive engineering came to an end, they continued to prosper.

Below: A French locomotive driver lubricates the complex valve gear of his Pacific locomotive. Although mechanical lubricators were gradually introduced, manual lubrication never disappeared.

Left: Slewing the track on a Chinese narrow-gauge forestry railroad.

Previous pages, page 202, above: Difficult and dangerous work: laying the Canadian Pacific tracks along the inhospitable north shore of Lake Superior in 1884.

Pages 202–03: The unusual triple-deck mobile dormitories used for construction workers of the railroad that was to become the Great Northern.

Page 203, above: Construction workers building a retaining wall and snowshed on the Canadian Pacific's line through Roger's Pass in the Rockies.

Above: Sometimes considerable finesse was required in placing ("spotting") a locomotive, notably on turntables where, for perfect balance, the locomotive had to be dead center.

Opposite: Grotesque accidents could result if rolling stock was moved when workers were engaged on it. Hence most railroad establishments were required to use this kind of portable warning sign.

Overleaf, page 206: The smokebox of a South African 4-8-4 is opened for a tube inspection.

Page 207: A Southern Pacific locomotive fitted for fire-fighting. Many railroads kept these, and trained men to use them. They were mainly intended to quell line-side blazes caused by locomotive sparks.

Left: Most large passenger stations had a train examiner who would tap train wheels with a hammer; a cracked wheel produced a muffled note.

Opposite, above: India's Railway Protection Force was intended to protect valuable shipments. Russia had a similar force, the Transport Armed Militia.

Opposite, below: A member of the British Transport Police, almost indistinguishable from the ordinary "bobby" but with a specialized role.

Below: In a British freight yard, two yardsmen confer with the locomotive driver. Each carries the tool of his trade, the shunting pole for manipulating the hook-and-chain couplings.

Opposite: The steam age was the age of friction bearings, and the oil can was everywhere. Lubrication needed to be both faultless and frequent; if it was not, a train fire could result.

Below: Despite appearances, attending to this American bar-framed 2-8-0 was less arduous than similar work on a British-style locomotive.

Bottom: Using a manual turntable in France. By the end of the steam age most turntables were powered, but unassisted turntables could still be found on branch lines.

Overleaf, page 212, above: A Canadian National brakeman in the 1950s. He is guiding the locomotive engineer in a backing movement.

Page 212, below: A late survival of American-style rooftop brakemen seen here on the Cuzco & Santa Ana Railway in Peru.

Page 213: At Salisbury, a British crew-changing point, the retiring crew give a hand in pushing the coal forward. Poor-quality coal like this was the bane of British locomotive crews in the 1950s.

Above: When grade crossings were frequent, an American engineer might keep his hand on the whistle cord for long stretches.

Opposite: Colorado, and to a lesser extent neighboring New Mexico, were once the home of several narrow-gauge railroads, and a few of these survive. This is a scene on the Cumbres & Toltec Railroad, which operates in both states.

Right: A Chinese locomotive driver with his oil can.

Overleaf, page 216: A Southern Pacific Railroad ticket office, in a carefully composed publicity picture.

Page 217: A Pullman porter at work in an open sleeper on the New York Central Railroad. The picture dates from the 1920s, but the hard work involved in this job did not diminish with the introduction of more modern rolling stock.

Steam Trains Preserved

The preservation movement, centered around the steam locomotive, has blossomed since the end of normal steam traction. But its roots go further back, to the nineteenth century, when the odd historic locomotive was put into a museum or on a pedestal. The first railway museum may have been that of St. Petersburg, dating from the 1840s, but this did not have any full-size locomotive exhibits. Major locomotive displays, including locomotives preserved long before the end of steam was envisaged, are offered by many specialized museums, of which the best-known are the Baltimore & Ohio, Pennsylvania State, and California State railroad museums and the St. Louis transportation museum in the United States; the National Railway Museum at York, England; the museum at Lucerne, Switzerland; and the Utrecht, Mulhouse, and Nuremburg rail museums in the Netherlands, France, and Germany.

Nowadays preservation takes a variety of forms, mostly linked to the tourist or "heritage" industry. One of the lessons learned by those who first preserved and organized steam railroads was that while enthusiasts provided an indispensable source of free labor, they were not numerous enough to form a market. Therefore, to pay their way, the preserved railroads needed to become tourist railroads. The most prosperous of the steam lines are those that are in tourist areas or within easy reach of big cities.

Steam tourist lines are usually owned by their operating company, but they sometimes operate over disused or little-used trackage. Often they consist of a preserved installation like a locomotive depot with some trackage over which a "live" locomotive can be run. The Spencer railroad workshops in North Carolina form one such example, as do the Carnforth and Didcot locomotive depots in Britain. More recently, Steamtown at Scranton, Pennsylvania, has been developed on this theme.

Preservation enterprises range from large organizations owning a dozen or more locomotives and running perhaps ten return trips at peak periods over lines that might be 10 miles or longer, down to a locomotive group possessing a single unrestored locomotive, a few yards of track, optimistic hopes for the future but little headway for the moment. The number of preserved steam locomotives throughout the world is astonishingly high, although most are museum pieces rather than operable machines. In the 1970s it was estimated that the United States and Britain each had about 1,500 such locomotives, and the number is unlikely to have changed much since then.

Opposite: On the *Durango & Silverton Narrow Gauge Railroad* in Colorado, a line that passes through dramatic Rocky Mountain terrain like the Animas Gorge, seen here.

Other countries are less fortunate. In France there were valiant efforts at preservation but too few people were involved. In Soviet Russia government-inspired scrap drives meant that historic locomotives unofficially marked for preservation were sent to the furnaces instead. In countries where steam traction ended after other countries had shown the possibilities of preservation the picture was happier. Australia, South Africa, and New Zealand are among these. In Germany, popular interest in steam locomotives and the prolonged use of main-line steam traction in what was then Communist East Germany provided a foundation for a healthy preservation movement.

In general, it is the English-speaking world that has led the way in modern-style railroad preservation. A landmark was the reorganization in 1950 of a Welsh narrow-gauge line, the Tallylyn Railway. This company was about to close because of lack of business, and a group of enthusiasts decided to resurrect it as a tourist railway. Having not only willing voluntary workers but also experts in many fields, this group was soon successful in attracting vacationers to its passenger trains. However, chances of imitating this success with a standard-gauge line were not highly rated, because such a line would be more expensive to operate. Nevertheless, another group of enthusiasts took over an abandoned British Railways branch in Sussex and this, the Bluebell Railway, also became a success both in financial terms (that is, paying its way) and in its preservation of the substance and atmosphere of a traditional British steam railway.

Other British ventures followed. Many of these are quite small, often concentrating on one particular facet of the past,

while others have developed into substantial enterprises. The Welsh narrow-gauge lines, where it all started, formed a distinct group, which decided to cooperate in "Great Little Trains of Wales" publicity; they are so close together that they can be offered as a combined tourist attraction. Among them is the Ffestiniog Railway, which in the nineteenth century was famed as a successful narrow-gauge line; under its new regime, it still is.

Just over the Welsh border in central England is the Severn Valley Railway, a large standard-gauge venture within reach of the densely populated Midlands and passing through a picturesque landscape. Other popular lines include the Keighley & Worth Valley in Yorkshire and the nearby North Yorkshire Moors Railway. Both these are in tourist regions; the K&WV has its main base a stone's throw from Haworth, a widely visited village because it was home to the literary Brönte sisters. In southern England, the Mid Hants Railway specializes in former Southern Railway equipment, while in the southwest the South Devon and the Torquay & Kingswear lines are strictly Great Western Railway style. Both the Isle of Man and the Isle of Wight have their steam railways, in the former case enjoying strong sponsorship from the local government with the 3ft-gauge line given as much publicity as the Manx cat, the island's well-loved mascot. In Scotland there are two lines still being developed; the Bo'ness Railway is within easy reach of Glasgow and Edinburgh, while the Strathspey Railway is in the center of a very scenic Highlands tourist region.

Steam railways are now very much part of the British heritage industry, and they have succeeded in maintaining a strong popular appeal without degrading the authenticity of their presentation. Several factors have helped in this. Britain is a small country, so few lines can be remote from a city or a tourist area. British amateurism could show itself at its best in this field, with many individuals willing to give time, money, and skills to projects. Importantly, one of the scrap metal dealers to whom British Railways disposed of its last steam locomotives proved cooperative in selling these derelict machines to enthusiast societies for restoration. This scrapyard was situated at Barry in South Wales, and received a preponderance of ex-Great Western locomotives, which is one reason why so many Great Western locomotives have been preserved.

In North America conditions were rather different, with states and railroads varying in their support, or lack thereof, for projects. What has emerged is a group of large and successful lines, together with very many others mainly of local interest only. Among the former is the Strasburg Railroad, which operates a former Pennsylvania RR branch line in the Amish tourist area. It has the advantage of adjoining another big railroad attraction, the Pennsylvania State Railroad Museum. Another Eastern standard-gauge line is that of the Valley RR in Connecticut, again thriving in a tourist area. The East Broad Top and the Cass Scenic railroads are associated with old

Below: A preserved British locomotive against the backdrop of the Yorkshire Dales. The "run-past" is a feature of many steam excursions, mainly for the benefit of photographers traveling on the train, who would otherwise have little chance of seeing the locomotive in action.

industries, and the latter has a fine collection of flexible-wheelbase locomotives formerly used for forestry work. Perhaps best-known of U.S. tourist lines is the Silverton RR, a narrow-gauge mountain line in Colorado, and there are other such lines operating in that state. In California a number of localities have resurrected sections of former forestry lines. In most states enthusiasts have set up museums, often in conjunction with running tracks or with excursions over main lines using their locomotives and rolling stock. Two of the biggest of these are at Union, Illinois, and Green Bay, Wisconsin.

The operation of main-line excursion trains hauled by preserved steam locomotives is a different aspect of preservation. Usually such excursions are one-time affairs requiring detailed planning. From year to year the routes and the locomotives change. Negotiations with the main-line railroad companies may be easy one

year, difficult the next. Lately, high insurance coverage has been needed, which has made many excursions financially unfeasible. For several years, the Norfolk Southern RR made two ex-Norfolk & Western locomotives available, but these have since been retired to a museum. Today the Union Pacific Railroad is a very supportive line, and trips behind its "Challenger" Mallet locomotive and its 4-8-4 No 844 are quite frequent.

In Britain, a commercial company operates its Pullman-car *Orient Express* train regularly out of London, normally behind a steam locomotive. There are also frequent scheduled steam trains from London to Stratford-on-Avon. In Scotland there are regular steam trips over the scenic West Highland Railway during the summer. Steam excursions by other organizations are also frequent, but these events are not straightforward to arrange. Railtrack, the track-owning company, does

Right: The Venice-Simplon Orient Express is a successful commercial venture reproducing the era of the international luxury train. It uses a set of restored Wagons-Lit cars in Continental Europe (as shown in this publicity picture), and Pullman cars for the English sector. The Pullman cars are also used for short steam-hauled excursions from London.

not want other trains delayed by late-running excursions, so limits the times and places where excursions can run. New safety regulations cast doubt on whether old rolling stock will be allowed on main lines. The replacement of vacuum by air brakes on British railways has been another problem. Lineside fires caused by locomotive sparks can be countered only by limiting excursions to the damp months, or equipping locomotives with spark arrestors or for burning oil, all of which demand time and money. But such excursions are the only way of demonstrating the capacity of the larger locomotives. A partial exception to this, however, is provided by the preserved Great Central Railway, which operates a length of former main line and does give scope for large locomotives to show their paces.

In the United States and Britain there are occasional major events in which preserved steam locomotives from several sources are combined into a dense program. In Britain the 150th anniversary of the Stockton & Darlington Railway was celebrated in this way, with exhibitions and parades of numerous locomotives. In the United States the annual conventions of the two major railroad historical societies also present a chance to display locomotives collected from all over the nation. In 1999 these displays were combined in the Sacramento Railfair, using the facilities of the California State Railroad Museum. Dozens of locomotives participated, and over the several days about 140,000 visitors attended. Such massive events cannot be frequent, but in both Britain and the United States more are planned.

Elsewhere in the world the preservation picture is patchy. Ireland has only a handful of preserved locomotives, but its preservationists make the best use of them by organizing each year trips lasting over a weekend and involving more than one locomotive. Such trips normally operate across the frontier dividing the two Irelands; the Irish Republic has most of the available trackage, while

Opposite: The "Skunk" of the California Western Railroad, which offers steam-hauled trips into the redwood forests of California from Fort Bragg. The line also carries a freight service.

the main base for preserved locomotives is near Belfast. Main-line steam excursions are a major attraction in Germany, where the national railway organizes a wide-ranging program each year, using preserved locomotives. The brochure detailing these excursions, which typically occur over the chosen routes at weekends through the summer months, can contain as many as forty-five pages. These excursions to some extent compensate for the infrequency of services on the privately preserved short lines. The latter are very numerous and sometimes use very interesting rolling stock, but most of them operate only a few days each year. For some reason, a mass tourist market for these short lines has not emerged in Germany.

In France, where there are only a handful of operable preserved locomotives, excursions are correspondingly rare. In recent years they have been hauled by a Chapelon Pacific and one of the American-built Mikado units. Privately preserved lines are also rare in France, but include the outstanding Vivarais Railway, which operates Mallet tank locomotives into the mountains of the *Massif Central*. There is also a standard-gauge line near Chinon in the Loire region, and a narrow-gauge line, the Baie de la Somme, not far from Calais.

Denmark and Sweden also are active in railroad preservation. In Austria the state railway uses steam haulage on a number of lines on certain days as a tourist attraction. There is also the narrow-gauge *Zillertalbahn*, serving a ski area. The Polish Railways maintain an all-steam locomotive depot at Wolsztyn; the steam locomotives haul normal scheduled trains and thereby attract a considerable number of tourists, especially from nearby Germany.

Russia, after a late start, is organizing a narrow-gauge tourist line at Pereslavl, in a historic area not far from Moscow.

Both Australia and New Zealand have several preserved lines and also operate steam excursions. New Zealand, soon after the end of steam, introduced the regular "Kingston Flyer," and the picture has developed since then. In Australia, the New South Wales Railway Museum south of Sydney not only houses locomotives but also operates trains with them. In the same state the former zigzag main line through the Blue Mountains has been converted to 3ft 6in gauge and runs, among others, former locomotives of the Queensland Railways. South Australia has a regular broad-gauge operation at Port Victor and a 3ft 6in-gauge service offered by the Pichi Richi Railway. In Victoria, the Puffing Billy narrow-gauge railway near Melbourne uses the tank locomotives of American design that were once so common in that state. All the states have their railway museums, and often run steam excursions. The museum train concept is also kept alive in Australia, with old locomotives hauling exhibition cars to celebrate centenaries of various townships and other events. In South Africa, where steam traction is still used in industry, the George–Knysna branch on the east coast sees regularly scheduled steam trains, and the Transnet Heritage Foundation organizes frequent "steam safaris." Not far away, in Zimbabwe, one can travel to Victoria Falls in a train hauled by a Garratt locomotive. Canada has a locomotive museum near Montreal at Delson; the long-lived Prairie Dog steam operation at Winnipeg, Manitoba; and a former Canadian Pacific "Royal Hudson" locomotive hauling regular trips for tourists out of Vancouver.

Previous pages: Another picturesque location on the Durango & Silverton Railroad, where the train skirts the Animas River near Silverton, Colorado. The line is of 3ft gauge, the narrow gauge most favored by American engineers. The lure of steam locomotives, the spectacular scenery, and deft publicity combine to make the Silverton line a top U.S. tourist attraction.

Opposite: A close-up of No. 480, one of the Durango & Silverton's 2-8-2 locomotives. This is of the K-36 type, built in the 1920s with the small driving wheels (44 inches) needed for mountain climbing.

Below: Another view of No. 480. Ten of this class of locomotive were built, by Baldwin, and most are still in service on the Durango & Silverton and Cumbres & Toltec Railroads.

Below: Taking on water on the Cumbres & Toltec Railroad. Jointly owned by the states of Colorado and New Mexico, this is a preserved section of what was once a much longer narrow-gauge line of the Denver & Rio Grande Western Railroad. It was the last U.S. narrow-gauge line to operate a named passenger train, the "San Juan," which ran between Alamosa and Durango.

Above: One of the K-36 class 2-8-2 locomotives of the Cumbres & Toltec Railroad. If the line is still under snow when train service begins in May, three of these locomotives are needed to propel the snowplow.

Overleaf: A view of the Cumbres & Toltec Railroad, whose 64-mile 3ft-gauge line crosses and recrosses the Colorado/New Mexico state line. The railroad operates from May through early October each year. During this period passengers have a chance to enjoy the celebrated aspen trees, whose fresh green leaves turn golden in the late summer. The "foliage excursion" has been a feature of American, and especially Canadian, railroads for decades, the fall being the favorite season.

Above: As well as running regular freight services, the Yolo Shortline Railroad of Woodland, California, also offers holiday and weekend steam excursions. This is one of its excursion trains, hauled by a former Southern Pacific Railroad six-wheel switcher.

Opposite: A meticulously restored 4-4-0 on view at Carson City, Nevada. The Nevada State Railroad Museum at Carson City specializes in relics of nineteenth-century Western railroads; as some of its locomotives are in working condition, it organizes occasional steam days.

Overleaf: A 4-4-0 displayed to commemorate the driving of the Last (or "Golden") Spike, which marked the link-up between the Central Pacific and Union Pacific Railroads to create America's first transcontinental line. The Union Pacific locomotive that took part in the 1869 ceremony was No 119, *Jupiter*.

Opposite: Engine 2102 belongs to a class of 4-8-4 freight locomotives built in 1945 by the Reading Railroad in its own workshops. In the 1960s this locomotive hauled some of the pioneer steam excursions, but it now works on the Blue Mountain & Reading Railroad in Pennsylvania. In this picture it is hauling an extra water tank; one of the problems of operating steam excursions is the disappearance of locomotive watering facilities.

Below: The Valley Railroad, which is based at Essex, Connecticut, offers combined train and river trips for tourists and steam enthusiasts. The railroad owns 2-8-0 and 2-6-2 locomotives that were acquired from various short lines. This picture shows one of the 2-6-2 locomotives, built by Baldwin in 1925.

Left: On the Llangollen Railway, a standard-gauge line in central Wales. A former Great Western tank locomotive prepares to leave the terminal.

Opposite: The Keighley & Worth Valley Railway in Yorkshire is one of Britain's most successful preserved lines. Here a double-chimney ten-wheeler, built by British Railways, handles the passenger service.

Below: *City of Truro* is part of Britain's "National Collection," by virtue of a record-breaking run with the "Ocean Mail" from Plymouth in 1904. It is seen here operating on loan to the Severn Valley Railway.

Opposite, above: One of the six London & North Eastern Railway's streamlined Pacifics that survived into preservation. This is *Union of South Africa*, hauling a steam excursion on the Settle & Carlisle line in northern England. Another member of this class, *Dwight D. Eisenhower*, went to the National Railroad Museum at Green Bay, Wisconsin, while yet another, *Dominion of Canada*, is at the Railway Historical Museum near Montreal.

Opposite, below: Another scene on the Settle & Carlisle line. The locomotive is the 2-10-0 *Evening Star*, the last steam locomotive built for British Railways.

Below: Locomotives on the North Yorkshire Moors Railway, another well-loved British tourist line. The engine shown hauling the morning passenger train out of Grosmont Tunnel is a six-wheel saddle-tank locomotive of the former Great Northern Railway. The steam trains and beautifully preserved station draw throngs of tourists each year to Grosmont, a traditional small town in which time seems almost to have stood still.

Opposite, above: England's Kent & East Sussex Railway specializes in small tank locomotives. One of them, a Brighton Line "Terrier," is shown here passing through the pastoral landscape that surrounds this line.

Opposite, below: A Mallet-type tank locomotive in operation on one of the meter-gauge lines still kept open in what was once the German Democratic Republic. The Mallet flexible-wheelbase locomotive was originally devised precisely for this kind of line.

Below: Dyed-in-the-wool rail fans may deplore this style of passenger vehicle, but Pennsylvania's Strasburg Railroad uses authentic rolling stock as well. The locomotive is a former Canadian National yard switcher.

Above: On the Zillertal Railway, one of several narrow-gauge steam lines in Austria. Most are of 2ft 6in gauge, although two mountain rack railways use the meter gauge. Because this part of the Tyrol is also a winter resort, trains run on this line throughout the year. The railway also offers a self-drive locomotive.

Below: Although German tourist lines operate excursions infrequently, several large static displays of steam locomotives are open year round. Some of these are based at old steam locomotive depots, as in this picture.

Opposite, above: On the Puffing Billy line near Melbourne, Australia. The locomotive is of the 2ft 6in-gauge U.S. design, which was widely used on the narrow-gauge railways of Victoria.

Below: A main-line steam excursion leaves Brussels, Belgium, hauled by a streamlined 4-4-2 locomotive. This unorthodox inside-cylinder design was intended for high-speed trains, but these never materialized because of the intervention of World War II. Belgian Railways operate several main-line excursions each year.

Opposite, below: Two preserved 4-4-0 locomotives of New South Wales Government Railways leave Sydney, Australia. They are hauling the state's "Vintage Train," although the first two vehicles are carrying locomotive water.

Opposite, above: Another view of the Pithiviers Railway, showing a train entering the terminus at Pithiviers. A traditional French checkerboard signal (the equivalent of the semaphore used by other railways) is in the foreground.

Opposite, below: A ten-wheeler of Prussian design takes out a local train of double-deck cars at Wolsztyn, Poland, where regular trains are hauled by steam locomotives retained in service for the purpose. On the right, a heavy freight locomotive, also of Prussian design, awaits repair.

Above: On the Pithiviers Railway in France. The locomotive has been uncoupled at the outer end of the line. This 2ft-gauge railway is a remnant of the portable "Décauville" lines that were used in French agriculture, especially for the beet industry, and by the French army as front-line supply railways.

Index

Page numbers in **boldface** refer to captions and illustrations.

ACKNOWLEDGMENTS

The publisher would like to thank the following individuals for their assistance in the preparation of this book: Robin Langley Sommer and Sara Hunt, editors; Nicola J. Gillies, photo editor; Charles J. Ziga, art director; Nikki L. Fesak, graphic designer; Lisa Langone Desautels, indexer; and the following people for their research, advice, and general assistance: Debby Cooper, Marilyn Holnsteiner, Marcie Johnson, Jerry Jordak, and Dan LeMaire.

PHOTO CREDITS

Every effort has been made to acknowledge the copyright owners of the photographs, as listed below with the page numbers on which they appear; if any errors are found, the publisher apologizes and will correct them in any future editions. The following institutions and individuals kindly gave permission for reproduction: © **Larry Angier**: 66, 67, 152, 153b, 160, 161b, 165t, 204b, 205, 210t, 211, 214, 234; **Peter Arnold, Inc.**: 6; 165b (© James L. Amos), 239 (© James L. Amos); **D.E. Cox Photo Library/ ChinaStock**: 54 (© Dennis Cox), 148 (© George Chan); © **Janelco Photographers**: 74–75 (© Eliot Cohen); © **Kathleen Norris Cook**: 218, 229; © **Ed Cooper Photo**: 70; © **2000 Dr. E.R. Degginger**: 238; © **Robert Drapala**: 177; © **Carolyn Fox**: 43b, 58, 135, 172, 173, 192–93, 231, 236–37; © **Winston Fraser**: 161t; © **A. Heywood**: 19b, 34t, 35b; © **Rudi Holnsteiner**: 34b, 71, 120t, 134 (both), 138–39, 139b, 142t, 164, 169, 246; © **Dave G. Houser**: 42, 47, 55; © **Kerrick James Photography**: 2, 59, 62–63, 225, 226–27, 230, 232–33; © **Wolfgang Kaehler**: 79 (both), 181, 188 (both); © **Dan LeMaire**: 92 (both), 93, 124t, 196, 197, 200; © **Joe McDonald**: 85; **OKAPIA**: 50 (© Bernd Kunz), 51 (© K. Wanecek), 247 (© Reinhard Schuster); © **Chuck Place**: 84, 215t; © **Larry Proser Photography**: 235; © **Connie Toops**: 121b; © **Stephen Trimble**: 184–85, 228; **Collection of John Westwood**: 1, 4, 10, 11, 12, 13, 14, 15 (both), 18, 21, 22, 23, 26 (both), 27t, 32–33, 35t, 36, 37, 38, 39, 40, 41 (both), 43t, 44, 45, 46, 48, 49 (both), 52–53 (all), 56 (both), 57, 60–61b, 61t, 64–65 (all), 68, 69 (both), 72, 73 (both), 78, 80 (both), 82b, 86–87, 88, 89 (both), 90 (both), 91, 94b, 95, 97, 98 (both), 99, 104, 108–109 (both), 110t, 111t, 116b, 121t, 124b, 125 (both), 127, 128b, 129, 130, 131 (both), 132, 133, 136, 137, 142b, 143, 144–5t, 144b, 145b, 146–47, 149 (both), 150–51 (both), 153t, 154–55b, 155 (both), 157, 158, 159, 166–67 (both), 168t, 175t, 179t, 180 (both), 183 (both), 186, 187, 189, 195, 198 (both), 199b, 201, 204t, 206, 208 (both), 209 (both), 210b, 212 (both), 213, 215, 221, 223, 240 (both), 241, 242 (both), 243, 244–45, 248, 249 (both), 250–51 (both); © **Charles J. Ziga**: 156, 168b, 176 (both); **Association of American Railroads**: 24t, 128t; **Burlington Northern Railway**: 202–203b; **Canadian Pacific Corporate Archives**: 107, 114, 174, 175b, 191b, 202, 203t; **Connecticut Historical Society**: 140b; **Greater London Record Office**: 182 (77/8997); **Hays T. Watkins Research Library, Baltimore & Ohio Railroad Museum**: 28–29t; **Kent Arts and Libraries, London**: 20, 24b, 106, 120b, 163, 199t; **Library of Congress, Prints & Photographs Division**: 8, 9, 16, 19t, 25, 30 (both), 100, 102, 112b, 113, 123, 126, 140t, 141, 178, 207, 216, 222; **National Archives**: 28–29b, 31, 60t, 76–77 (both), 82–83t, 94t, 103, 118, 119, 170–71b, 170t, 179b, 21; **New York Central System Historical Society**: 110–11b; **Courtesy of the New York Historical Society, New York City**: 162 (#50219); **Planet Art**: 116tr & tl; **Santa Fe Railway**: 81, 122; **Science and Society Picture Library, London**: 96, 117 (both); **Special Collections, University of Arizona Library**: 101, 115; **Southern Pacific Railroad Bulletin**: 194; **Union Pacific Railroad Museum Collection**: 105, 112t, 170t, 190, 191t.